Case Studies in Business Data Bases

James Bradley

HOLT, RINEHART AND WINSTON, INC.
New York   Chicago   San Francisco   Philadelphia
Montreal   Toronto   London   Sydney   Tokyo

Requests for permission to make copies of any part of the work
should be mailed to:
Permissions
Holt, Rinehart and Winston, Inc.
111 Fifth Avenue
New York, NY 10003

Library of Congress Cataloging-in-Publication Data
Bradley, James, 1942-
   Case studies in business data bases.

   1. Business—Data bases—Case studies.   2. Data base
management—Case studies.   I. Title.
HF5548.2.B6778 1987   025'.0665   87-26597

ISBN 0-03-014134-6

Printed in the United States of America

8 9 0 1   039 9 8 7 6 5 4 3 2 1

Holt, Rinehart and Winston, Inc.
The Dryden Press
Saunders College Publishing

Case Studies in
Business Data Bases

2+4

Preface

When I was asked to write a second edition for my text *Introduction to Data Base Management in Business*, my editor also asked me for a book on case studies in data base management. The reasoning behind the request was simple. The case study approach is widely used in business, and many texts in business have associated case studies texts. A business data base text, therefore, ought to have an associated case studies text as well.

I believe this case studies text will be useful to instructor and student alike, no matter what data base text they use, because an important feature is its independence of any specific data base text; any of the current crop of data base texts may be used with it.

The book covers six cases. The first three cases are about small firms and are in order of increasing difficulty. These first three cases are unique because they deal with the whole firm, that is, the big picture. Furthermore, we see these cases through the eyes and experiences of a recently graduated data base analyst. Because we deal with the big picture, we run into a practical problem not covered in data base texts, namely the problem of incorporating accounting data into data bases without compromising the firm's accounting system. We tackle the accounting data problem head-on in these cases, but in a manner that is instructive even to those with only a hazy notion of accounting principles.

Dealing with data bases for the whole firm with smaller enterprises is an important educational approach. This forms a firm foundation for dealing with data bases for large organizations where only a portion of the operational business data is involved. The final three cases in the book deal with such noncomprehensive data bases. As a result, I believe that the cases dealt with in this book offer a totally different perspective on data bases in business, but also one that is necessary and practical.

The later three cases on data bases for larger organizations were chosen both for their diversity and for their ability to reinforce ideas and concepts learned from the first three cases for small businesses. In other words, they are supposed to integrate with the earlier cases where accounting data dominates. Readers can pick and choose among these latter cases, but should cover all the first three cases to get maximum benefit from the book.

I am grateful to my editors for insisting on this project, first Miles Thompson, and later Devilla Williams. I personally learned a great deal from it, and I am sure that those who study the cases described will also.

J. Bradley

Contents

Preface

Chapter One

Introduction *1*

Note on Diagrams for Conceptual Data Bases 5
Diagrams Without Fields 6
Diagrams With Fields 7

Chapter Two

LSI, Inc., Lost Vegas, Nevada *11*

Operation of LSI 11
Recording of Business Transactions for LSI, Inc. 14
A Data Base Design Task 15
LSI's Accounting System 17
Explanation of LSI's Accounting System 19
The Trial Balance 26
Revenue and Expenditure Accounts 28
Computer System Design 31
Files Versus Data Bases for LSI 32
The Proposed Data Base Design for LSI 33
Operation of the System 36
Computer System 39
Postscript 39
Questions 40

Chapter Three

Silicon Mountain Supplies, Inc.   *42*

Business Activities at SMS   45

SMS's Documentation System   48

Introduction to Data Base Management at
   SMS, Inc.   54

Computer System Design   56

Data Base Considerations   59

Data Base Design Options at SMS   61

Design of the Data Base for Parts, Sales and
   Purchases   62

Final Conceptual Data Base Design Steps   83

Data Base Design for the Remaining General Ledger
   Data Base   85

Check on Business Applicability of the Proposed
   Data Bases   88

Final Specifications and Implementation   90

Questions   91

Chapter Four

General Power, Inc.   *94*

Organization of General Power   95

Computer Systems at General Power   98

Data Analysis   99

Data Base Design   107

Preliminary Design Review   113

Extension of the Basic Data Base Designs   114

Data Base for Journal and Remaining General Ledger
   Accounts   116

A Fundamental Difficulty   120

Sequel   121

Appendix: Balance Problems with the
   GP Data Bases   123

Questions   125

Chapter Five

American Electric, Inc.   *127*

The Design Steps   133

Questions   140

Chapter Six

Peryl-Links Securities, Inc. *142*

Common Stock File STOCK *149*
Corporate Bond File BOND *152*
Preferred Stock File PREFERRED *154*
Stock Warrant File WARRANT *155*
Convertible Bond File CONVERTIBLE-BOND *157*
The Convertible Preferred File CONVERTIBLE-
   PREFERRED *158*
Relationships *158*
Design of Views *163*
Accounting Data and Dependencies *167*
Final Design *171*
Questions *172*

Chapter Seven

Securities & Exchange Commission, Washington, D.C. *174*

Mergers and Acquisitions *176*
Data Base for Takeovers *178*
Data Base for Amalgamations *184*
Concluding Steps *186*
Questions *187*

Case Studies in Business Data Bases

ONE

Introduction

The principles behind data bases and data base management systems for the operational data of business, although still evolving, are by now probably well-established, and there are many excellent texts on the subject. Although practically all texts agree as to the core of the subject, there is a wide diversity of opinion as to how the subject should be approached and taught. Nevertheless, every single text with which the author is familiar is lacking in one fundamental aspect—the treatment of accounting data.

It is clear that data base systems can be used for purposes other than the operational data of business—for example, the management of data bases in engineering. However, when we look at the operational data of business, accounting data predominates. But accounting data must fit into an accounting system for the firm; that is, a system set up by the firm's accountants involving journals and ledgers.

So here we have a very practical problem, which comes to the fore whenever we look at practical cases of operational data management in business. How do we incorporate accounting data into business data bases? Remarkably, there appears to be no broadly-based theory as to how this should be done. Although it is done in practice every day in business, none of the standard accounting texts currently have anything to say about data bases and data base systems. And none of the current crop of data base textbooks have anything to say about accounting systems.

Accounting systems go back a long time. Modern accounting systems are all derived from the accounting equation and the concept of double-entry bookkeeping, which originated with Florentine merchants in Italy as long ago as the fourteenth century. Accounting science has fundamentallyy changed very little since those early days, although there have been many refinements with changing times. Data base principles, on the other hand, are very recent, dating from the last third of the twentieth centry, and they are still evolving.

Data base and accounting systems both appear to have evolved as a result of practical experience in business, and as time goes on we can expect that accounting and data base practice will greatly influence each other. Thus we are all still learning. But when there is a conflict between the two, it seems to this author that, for the present, the data base specialist must bow to the principles of accounting. Six hundred years of evolution and satisfactory service to business by accounting must be treated with respect. In practice, this means that if there is a conflict between data base and accounting practice, it is wiser to give the accounting practice the benefit of the doubt. And as we shall see in the case studies in this book, such conflicts do occur.

One way to avoid the problem of the integration of accounting and data base principles is to consider data bases for only smaller segments of a firm's operations, so that the operational data managed by the data base system and the accounting data in the general ledger accounts are largely, if not completely, independent of each other. This is the approach taken in most texts and to some extent in business practice—where you can get away with it. In many texts you can find conceptual files that have accounts receivable data, or accounts payable data, or fixed assets data, but, at least so far, you will not find any of these data base texts dealing with the fact that if there is an update to accounts receivable, for example, there has to be an update to some other account, in accordance with accounting principles.

The problem for the data base textbook authors is that there simply is not space to cover accounting principles in their text, nor can they assume a working knowledge of accounting on the part of the readers. Accordingly, they all do the only practical thing and simply ignore accounting systems. The accounting textbook authors have clearly the converse problem, and they in turn stick with accounting and ignore data bases.

In developing cases in business data base management the temptation to continue the data base tradition of ignoring the accounting aspect of things is great. Unfortunately, this is very difficult to do, for a fundamental reason: cases in data base management in business tend to be very specialized and involved if they are truly to reflect business reality. The typical design and implementation of just one business data base could fill many hundreds of pages without exhausting it. As a result, the case writer is forced to begin with cases for smaller firms, where the circumstances of the case can be more readily pinned down. But when you deal with business data bases for a small firm you come right up against accounting systems, which simply cannot be ignored.

There is a positive aspect to this difficulty. From an educational point of view, the student of data base management is better off to begin with comprehensive data bases for smaller firms, and later transfer the insight gained to work on data bases for larger firms, where a single data base will hold only a fraction of the firm's important data. This, of course, is the old crawl-before-you-walk approach.

After much research, we decided to go for this crawl-before-you-walk approach, involving a head-on assault on the accounting systems/data base problem.

The idea behind the case studies in this book is thus quite simple. The first three cases deal with comprehensive data bases for smaller firms. The skills and knowledge acquired from these three cases are then used with the specialized data bases for large organizations, described in the subsequent three cases.

With the first three cases for the small firms, we start with a simple firm, where one data base covers everything. The second firm is slightly more complex and requires two data bases. The third firm is even more complex and requires three data bases.

The first three cases for the small firms are interrelated. One of the data bases for the second firm turns out to be the same as that for the first firm. And the data bases used in the third case are all major modifications of the two data bases used with the second case. With all three cases, we keep very close to the accounting system used with the operational data.

Seen from an accounting point of view, the first case involves straight cash accounting, with no receivables. Neither is there any manufacturing to complicate things. The second case involves receivables and payables, but still no manufacturing. The third and most complex case involves receivables, payables, and manufacturing (which means incoming parts inventory and outgoing finished goods inventory).

These three cases are covered in the form of a narrative of the problems and experiences of a recently graduated data base systems analyst called Sarah Didjet, who is knowledgeable about data bases but has forgotten most of the accounting she ever learned. But Sarah learns—from experience. She works for a systems firm in San Francisco, called Cybertek International, and the three cases involve firms that are clients of Cybertek. It is Sarah who is assigned to the three firms.

The first firm, called LSI, Inc., of Lost Vegas, Nevada, is trivially simple, but even here the accounting manages to give Sarah some headaches. The second firm, called Silicon Mountain Supplies, Inc., of San Jose, is an electronics parts wholesaler, which forces Sarah to learn about receivables, payables and inventory. The third firm, called General Power, Inc., is a manufacturer of equipment using a wide variety of parts, and it causes Sarah to come to grips with the problems of receivables, payables, assets, depreciation, parts inventory, finished goods inventory, and more.

Sarah's experiences in dealing with the whole firm in these three cases give her a solid foundation for later projects where she will deal with only a portion of a very large organization. She has learned to see things in the light of the overall picture. And, it is to be hoped, so will the reader.

The latter three case studies in the book have to do with a national industrial concern, with a national securities firm, and with the S.E.C., a regulatory arm of the U.S. Government. Because these case studies deal with large organizations, they necessarily take the form of an overview and do not get too detailed. The particular cases were chosen to reinforce the knowledge gained from the first three cases.

Note on Diagrams for Conceptual Data Bases

When designing data bases, the conceptual data base is designed first. We refer to a conceptual data base in the context of the ANSI/SPARC 3-level architecture. Frequently diagrams are used to communicate tentative conceptual data bases. A number of diagrammatic techniques are in common use. In this book we use both conventional and extended Bachman diagrams. The other most popular type of diagram is the entity-relationship diagram or E-R diagram. Our only reason for using Bachman diagrams is that they are more suitable for a book, since they take up much less space than E-R diagrams. However, for the benefit of readers who are not using Bachman diagrams in their course text, the following should explain how the various types of diagram relate to each other.

We use two examples of conceptual files, one for 1:n relationships, and the other for many-to-many (n:m) relationships:

(a) Conteptual files for the 1:n relationship

1. A file called WAREHOUSE, where each record describes a warehouse belonging to a firm. The fields are:

WHNUMB	warehouse number, primary key
CITY	city containing the warehouse
FLOORS	number of floors in the warehouse

2. A file called EMPLOYEE, where each record describes an employee working at the firm. The fields are:

WHNUMB	the warehouse at which the employee works
EMPNUMB	the employee number, primary key
SALARY	the employee's salary
YEAR	the year the employee was hired

There is a 1:n relationship between WAREHOUSE and EMPLOYEE, since for one warehouse, there may be many employees working in that warehouse, whereas for one employee, there is only one warehouse at which an employee works.

(b) Conceptual files for n:m relationship

1. The EMPLOYEE file, as above.
2. A file called SUPPLIER, where each record describes a supplier. The fields are:

SNUMB	supplier number, primary key
SNAME	name of supplier (company name)
LOC	state in which supplier is headquartered

3. A file called PUR-ORDER, where each record describes the quantity of items ordered from a supplier by an employee. The fields are:

EMPNUMB	employee number of employee who issued the order
SNUMB	supplier number of supplier who was given the order
ORDERNUMB	identification number for the order, primary key
QTY	quantity of items ordered

There is a 1:n relationship between EMPLOYEE and PUR-ORDER, since an employee can issue many purchase orders and a purchase order has to be issued by some one employee. There is also a 1:n relationship between SUPPLIER and PUR-ORDER, since a supplier can get many orders, and an order must be for some one supplier. This means that there is a many-to-many relationship between EMPLOYEE and SUPPLIER, since an employee will issue orders to many suppliers, and a supplier can receive orders from many employees.

Diagram Without Fields

You can show the structure of a conceptual data base by showing just the conceptual files and the relationships between them, without any fields. This is illustrated in Figure 1.1 for the 1:n relationship between WAREHOUSE and EMPLOYEE. In (a) we have a Bachman diagram, where the arrow points to the child or "many" file of a 1:n relationship. In (b) and (c) the

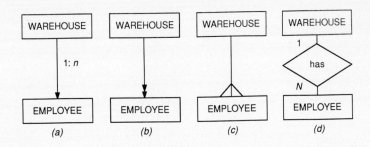

FIGURE 1.1. Methods of displaying a 1:n relationship between two conceptual files. The entity-relationship diagram in d signifies that a warehouse has many employees.

double arrow and the crow's foot indicate the "many" conceptual file. In (d) we have an E-R diagram, which uses a diamond with a relationship name, such as "has", to indicate a 1:n relationship. Note also the positions of the 1 and N. The N denotes the "many" file. Usually the name used in the diamond is chosen to be meaningful to nontechnical persons. Thus a warehouse "has" many employees.

The E-R diagram for displaying the many-to-many relationship between EMPLOYEE and SUPPLIER is shown in Figure 1.2a. The many-to-many relationship is indicated by a (relationship) diamond inside a (file) box. The relationship is given a meaningful name, such as ORDERS FROM. The box indicates that a conceptual file will be needed for this relationship. Note the N and the M at EMPLOYEE and SUPPLIER. Where a 1:n relationship is displayed as an E-R diagram, sometimes a lower case name is used (Figure 1.1) to indicate that the relationship will not give rise to a separate conceptual file. The Bachman diagram for the many-to-many relationship is shown in Figure 1.2b. This diagram brings out the fact that a many-to-many relationship decomposes into two 1:n relationships.

Diagrams With Fields

We can add fields to the diagram shown above. In the case of E-R diagrams we simply add a bubble for each field in a file, as

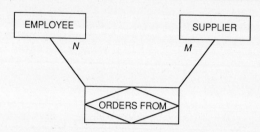

(a) Entity-relationship diagram for the many-to-many relationship between conceptual files EMPLOYEE and SUPPLIER (vendor). ORDERS FROM is a conceptual file or relation, but it also carries the information about the relationship between EMPLOYEE and SUPPLIER. As such, ORDERS FROM is special and is given a special box. In addition, the name tells us something about the relationship, in that employees order from suppliers.

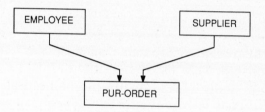

(b) With Bachman and similar diagrams, no special attempt is made to distinguish the conceptual file or relation PUR-ORDER that carries the information about the many-to-many relationship between EMPLOYEE and SUPPLIER.

FIGURE 1.2.

shown for the 1:n relationship between WAREHOUSE and SUPPLIER in Figure 1.3a. In the case of the Bachman diagram, we simply expand the boxes to include the fields (Figure 1.3b). Note that it is usual to underscore the primary key field. In addition, it is common to let the 1:n relationship arrow begin at the primary key field of the parent file (WAREHOUSE) and end on the foreign key (or connection field) of the child file (EMPLOYEE); the foreign key field is said to support the relationship.

In the case of the many-to-many relationship, we add fields to the E-R diagram with bubbles as before (Figure 1.4a), except that

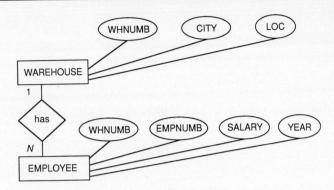

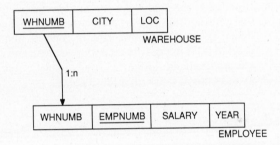

(a) Entity-relationship diagram, showing fields, for the 1:n relationship between WAREHOUSE and EMPLOYEE.

(b) (Extended) Bachman diagram for the 1:n relationship between WARE-HOUSE and EMPLOYEE. Note that the 1:n arrow begins on the primary key field WHNUMB of the parent WAREHOUSE file, and ends on the foreign key of the child EMPLOYEE file. The diagram thus shows what fields directly support the 1:n relationship.

FIGURE 1.3.

this time, we must add field bubbles to the relationship box, since this will be implemented as a conceptual file. The fields for the many-to-many Bachman diagram are shown in Figure 1.4b.

The diagrams in Figures 1.1b and 1.1c may be expanded to show fields much like Bachman diagrams. Bachman diagrams with fields and arrows ending on foreign keys are sometimes called *extended Bachman diagrams*.

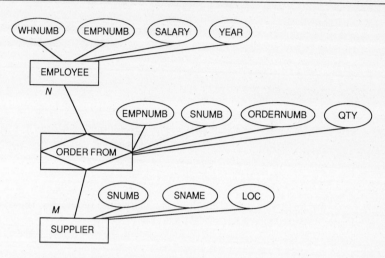

(a) How fields are depicted in an entity-relationship diagram. In a preliminary design this type of diagram allows easy addition and deletion of
fields, as the design proceeds. In contrast, the extended Bachman diagram in (b) is not easy to alter, once drawn, and so it is better for showing
a more finalized design. A disadvantage of the entity-relationship diagram is that it takes up a lot of space.

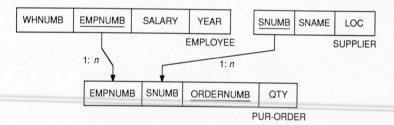

(b) Extended Bachman diagram for the many-to-many relationship between
EMPLOYEE and SUPPLIER. This diagram not only gives the field name,
but points out the primary keys and the foreign keys or connection fields
supporting the 1:n relationships implicit in the many-to-many relationship.

FIGURE 1.4.

TWO

LSI, Inc.,
Lost Vegas, Nevada

Joe Sharp owns and operates LSI, Inc., located in the city of Lost Vegas, Nevada. The firm was originally called Lucky Strike Industries, Inc. Joe's parents came to Nevada as children during the famous Nevada gold boom in the early part of the century. They never did find much gold, but their son Joe struck it rich with LSI. You see, LSI is something of a gold mine to it's owner. It is a casino.

Now before we go any farther, let it be known that this case writer does not approve of casinos, and never goes near them; readers will stay away from them too, if they value their financial health.

Nevertheless, Joe's business is interesting because of its sheer simplicity. It has no receivables, no payables, and even no fixed assets. But, as you might expect, with understandable disapproval, it does generate a lot of cash. The simplicity of Joe's business makes it relatively easy to examine the practical end of how computers and data bases may be used for the fundamentals of keeping track of accounting data in business.

Operation of LSI

Joe likes to keep things simple, and his business could not be simpler. Besides himself, two other people work for LSI. First there is the doorkeeper, known as Big Ed. Ed's job is to ensure that dress codes are complied with in the casino. (Ladies are expected to wear dresses, and gentlemen have to wear a jacket and tie. Jeans are definitely out. LSI is a high-class establishment.) The other employee is Lucy, who works in the office.

The establishment has only two main rooms, and is located inside the Lost Vegas Halltone Hotel, just right of the main lobby. To enter the first room, you must pass Big Ed's careful scrutiny. This first outer room is elegantly appointed, with soft carpets and easy chairs that you just sink into. Also in this outer room is a long counter, on the left. A plan of the establishment is shown in Figure 2.1. Lucy sits behind the counter, and

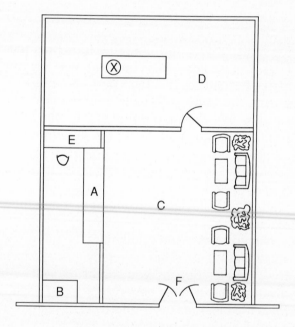

FIGURE 2.1.   LSI's establishment. Coming in through the main entrance F, you are in the outer room C. You buy and redeem chips from Lucy, who works behind the counter A. Lucy also has a desk at E, where she does the books for LSI. She keeps the firm's cash in the safe B. In the outer room C you can sit down, on the right. In the roulette room you have to stand. Normally, there is a large crowd standing around the roulette table in the inner room D.

exchanges dollars for plastic blue chips, and vice versa. You pay $10 dollars for a single chip, which is the minimum bet at the roulette table.

The average customer will have the following experience. He or she comes into the first room and gives Lucy about $100 in exchange for 10 blue chips. The customer then proceeds to the second, or inner, room where the roulette table is located. A large and impressive chandelier hangs down above the roulette table, which is usually surrounded by a richly dressed clientele. Joe is running the table. The average customer will win sometimes and lose sometimes. All too often the customer has lost his chips in only a few plays. A few do well and are able to cash in a small fortune in chips after hours of playing. Of those that lose, a few manage to avoid losing all their chips and are able to cash in the few remaining at Lucy's counter.

On a typical day, total sales of chips will be about $50,000 with redeemed chips amounting to about $46,000, a for gross profit of about $4,000 per day. There are days when Joe loses, but these are not common. The odds are slightly in favor of the house, so that the laws of averages working with large numbers of customers ensure Joe a profit. Joe is scrupulously honest, however. He has a prominent sign displayed above Lucy's counter, informing customers what the odds are. Few customers ever bother to read it.

Joe does have costs, but even here he is careful to keep things simple. Joe firmly believes that making money should be both simple and enjoyable. Both Lucy and Ed work for a service firm, called Heritage Management. Joe simply pays Heritage $1,000 per week for their services. That way Joe escapes having to worry about payroll deductions. Heritage looks after that.

The entire premises, including furniture (even the roulette table), are leased from the Lost Vegas Halltone Hotel for $20,000 per week. So Joe has no worries about depreciation, maintenance, or procurement of furniture. The hotel looks after that. (Incidentally, the hotel makes more money from Joe's lease than from all the other operations of the hotel put together!)

Joe has to keep rather large sums of cash on hand (in the safe behind Lucy's counter), to take care of the possibility of a big winner. Some of these funds are the firm's, but about half of them are short term loans from two local banks, the Lost Vegas Federated Bank (LVFB) and the Last National Bank (LNB). The banks send Joe a bill for interest every week. Joe has never missed a payment. Bank debt is about $50,000.

LSI is a corporation and has to pay taxes on its profits; it writes a check each quarter for taxes. Joe receives a salary from LSI of about $10,000 per month. This money is paid directly to Joe's accountant, who calculates the necessary deductions. The accountant then forwards personal income taxes and other deductions to the appropriate government departments and issues a check to Joe for the net. Thus the payroll processing for Joe is hidden from both Joe and LSI, which is the way we shall leave it.

Recording of Business Transactions for LSI, Inc.

LSI keeps a journal in which every financial transaction is recorded. To avoid having to record each sale of blue chips, and each redemption of chips, the total sales of chips for each day are recorded in the journal. The following indicates the common kinds of journal entries that can occur:

22/05/87	Chip sales	$55,000
22/05/87	Chip redemptions	$49,000
22/05/87	New loan from bank	$20,000
22/05/87	Loan repayment to bank	$25,000
22/05/87	Interest payment to bank	$ 800
22/05/87	Rent	$20,000
22/05/87	Heritage services	$ 1,000
22/05/87	Tax payment	$ 5,000
22/05/87	Personal salary withdrawal	$10,000

It is Lucy who records these transactions in the journal. Readers who have taken an elementary accounting course will recall that a business journal is nothing more than a chronologically ordered recording of business transactions.

At least once a week, Lucy also posts each transaction to the general ledger accounts. She does this posting using conventional double-entry bookkeeping—about which we will explain later. It is from the updated general ledger accounts that Lucy can extract the income statement for any period, such as a month, a quarter, or a year. The income statement simply shows revenues and expenditures for the period involved, and the difference between revenue and expenditure is the firms profit, or net earnings.

Lucy can also obtain the balance sheet at any point, usually month end. The balance sheet lists the firm's assets (asset side), and the firm's equity and liabilities (liability side), which shows who owns rights to the asssets. More about all this presently.

A Data Base Design Task

Joe makes a lot of money, as we have seen. Unfortunately, he never knows how much he is worth on any given day, or how much the firm has earned over any given period. He could in theory get this information from Lucy any time he wanted it. But in practice Lucy is very busy, and has time to calculate income statements and balance sheets only once a month. Joe would like to do better than that. For example, he would like to see daily graphical displays of revenues and expenditures (as in Figure 2.2a), and a daily graphical display of total assets and total liabilities (Figure 2.2b), as well as other current information displays.

For a long time Joe has felt that a computer could be used to keep track of his business information, and that all the facts and figures could be kept in a computer data base, to be extracted in a instant (or so he imagines) when needed. Because of the sensitive nature of his business, Joe has always felt that meticulous and impeccable record keeping was essential—you never could tell when some anti-this-or-that group would launch a campaign to have him shut down.

However, for a long time Joe had hesitated about computerizing his business. He knew his business was simple. But he also knew that computers were complicated things, and he was familiar with some of the horror stories about local businesses that had introduced computers. He also intensely disliked complexity. Nevertheless, Joe was becoming impressed with the stories about what a properly installed data base could do for him, so one day he visited a long established and reputable San Francisco firm of computer consultants, called Cybertek International, Inc., that had about 80 employees.

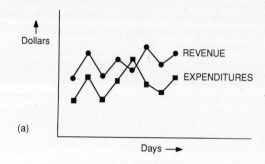

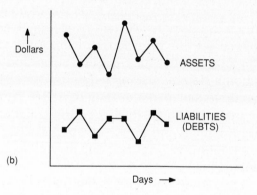

FIGURE 2.2. Joe Sharp would like to be able to get instant displays of the variation of financial quantities over time, such as those above.

Joe talked with Peter Stone, vice-president in charge of customer systems development. Peter listened attentively to Joe's description of his business, and particularly to what it was that Joe wanted. As Joe talked he made careful notes, and interrupted Joe only to get clarification of specific details.

When Joe had finished, Peter thought for a while. Finally he informed Joe that Cybertek would be willing to handle the job, and that what Joe wanted could be easily set up in about two months. He told Joe that he would send a young systems analyst called Sarah Didjet to visit LSI in Lost Vegas.

As soon as Joe has left the office, Peter lifted up the phone. "Miss Didjet," he said, "are you still interested in a job with Cybertek? Good, then you start tomorrow. Be in my office at 8 a.m. sharp. I'll explain your first assignment."

Then Peter went in to see the president of Cybertek, Joan Brayns, and told her how he was going to handle the LSI project. He told her that although he was not very happy to send someone straight out of college like Sarah Didjet, everyone else was busy with long term projects. He could not turn Joe down, he explained, for this was Cybertek's chance to get a foot in the door of some of the very large and lucrative businesses in Lost Vegas. "Everyone in Lost Vegas will know what kind of a job we do for Joe Sharp," he went on, "and we can easily check on each stage of Sarah Didjet's work, in case she's not quite up to it." Joan gave the project her blessing. Next day, Sarah Didjet was given a briefing by Peter Stone, and before she knew what was happening she was in Lost Vegas, being scrutinized for compliance with LSI's dress code by Big Ed at the entrance to LSI's casino.

LSI's Accounting System

Sarah began by becoming familiar with the actual business activities at LSI. She even played the roulette wheel with some chips provided free by Lucy, but like so many others she returned fewer chips to Lucy than she was given. Joe's end of the table, as always, attracted the chips like a magnet. Peter had told Sarah not to worry too much about the amount of time she spent, as it was more important to do an impressive job.

When she was fully informed about the operation of the business, and duly impressed by how much money it pulled in, Sarah had Lucy explain how the manual accounting system worked. Unfortunately, when Lucy began to get into double-entry bookkeeping, Sarah got lost. It had been four years since she had taken any accounting, a subject which she had not found very exciting. She was able to follow the details of each of the accounts in the general ledger, but somehow the overall picture eluded her. Fortunately, Lucy, who was impressed by the occasional remark by Sarah about "systems implications of specific transaction updates," did not discover that Sarah did not understand the overall manual system.

That evening just before dinner, Peter Stone called to keep tabs on developments. Sarah told him about how she had already become familiar with the business and how she had been going through the manual accounting system with Lucy. She said nothing about her difficulties comprehending the accounting the accounting system, but said that she thought that the answer was a single data base for all the firm's data with a matching processing system—something she had been taught is rarely possible with a large organization. She was relieved to hear that Peter confirmed her hunch. He said it was a good project for someone just starting out because it involved the entire picture. He went on to say that most business data bases and associated applications programs just deal with a part of the overall business and that few computer systems analysts ever get to understand how a large firm functions—from a financial and accounting point of view.

"In fact," he continued, "many company presidents don't understand that either, although our Joan Brayns certainly does. You know, I've seen company presidents with their firm in trouble, no liquid working capital to speak of, and creditors beating on the door, sitting there mystified by the firm's balance sheet, and asking accountants why they just can't make use of some of the apparently huge sums listed there. You're lucky to have this project. By the time you're finished with it you'll understand the fundamentals of meshing a firm's accounting system with its data bases. Things are not all as tidy as they appear in the data base text books; the truth of the matter is that it's an untidy world out there. Tidy things up at LSI as best you can. We're depending on you."

We're depending on you! And I can't even remember how-double entry bookkeeping works, thought Sarah as she ate that evening.

But Sarah was not one to refuse a challenge. Next morning at breakfast, she said to herself: I may not remember much about double-entry bookkeeping, but I did take a course in accounting; I'm sure it would all come back to me if I just had some time to myself with an elementary text on accounting. She decided to spend the morning in the business section of Lost Vegas City Library, brushing up on accounting. Her business at the library was very specific. She had to make sense of LSI's accounting system. So she took with her the notes she had made on LSI, plus some copies of pages from LSI's general ledger accounts and also from the journal.

That morning she worked hard, using an accounting text to help her draw diagrams of LSI's system. Finally, after about three hours, the whole thing was clear. The following material shows how Sarah came to understand the way LSI's system worked.

Explanation of LSI's Accounting System

To understand accounting systems it is best to start with the organization's balance sheet. A balance sheet gives two views of an organization, and we shall use LSI as an example. These two views are not the only views of the organization. For example, Figure 2.1 shows another view. Nevertheless, no matter how many different views we have of a business, these views are all describing different aspects of the same thing.

In Figure 2.3 we show LSI's balance sheet in diagrammatic form. The center column is the entity LSI, and you can imagine it any way you want. The left column shows the assets, in money terms, that go to make up LSI. LSI's assets are its cash, with cash on hand in Lucy's safe, and the rest in two demand deposit accounts at two different banks (LVFB and LNB). All this is illustrated by the asset column on the left.

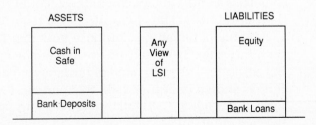

FIGURE 2.3. A balance sheet shows two quite different views of a company. The asset side or view show the value of each asset (physical thing) belonging to the firm. The liability side shows who has rights to those assets.

The column on the right gives another view of the firm, the ownership view, or who has the right to what. Some of LSI's cash is borrowed from the banks. These are the loans listed at bottom right. They are all long-term loans, but LSI has the right to pay them off any time it pleases. (Usually Joe cuts down on these loans when interest rates are high; he can also pay off only a portion of a loan if desired.) The rest of the column on the right shows how much of the assets belong to LSI; this is the equity portion.

The column on the left is known as the *asset side* of the balance sheet; that on the right is called the *liability side*, or *equity/liability* side. Now, since each side is describing different aspects of views of the same thing, namely LSI, and since the size of each is measured in dollars, each side must be the same size. This is fundamental, and if you are not familiar with it, pause to think about it.

A balance sheet is a snapshot of the firm at some instant. If we take a snapshot a shot while later, the balance sheet will be different, with the individual parts that make up the columns having changed size. Nevertheless, the left side will still be the same size as the right side, since, as always, the two sides are merely different aspects of the same thing.

This explains why double-entry bookkeeping is used in most accounting systems. Suppose that LSI takes out a new loan of $40,000 from LNB, the proceeds of which are placed in LSI's demand account at LNB. Both left and right sides of the balance sheet expand by $40,000, as illustrated in Figure 2.4a. If we keep an account to track loans (a liability account), an entry of $40,000 will have to be made in that account. We will also have to make an entry of $40,000 in the account that tracks demand deposits at LNB. Thus two entries are required.

As a further example, suppose now that Lucy goes to LNB, withdraws the $40,000 from the demand account, and places it in LSI's safe. The right hand of the balance sheet is not affected. But, as shown in Figure 2.4b, two parts of the left side change. First, the funds at LNB fall by $40,000, and second, the funds in the safe climb by $40,000, so that the total size of the asset side does not change, although its composition does. Again, the bookkeeper has to make an entry in each of two separate accounts, one to record the withdrawal from LNB and the other to record the placing of the funds in LSI's safe.

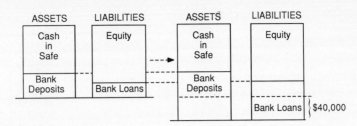

(a) Both sides are affected when a new loan is taken out (for $40,000).

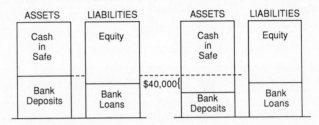

(b) Only the asset side is affected when the $40,000 is removed from a bank deposit and placed in LSI's safe.

FIGURE 2.4.

That, in a nut shell, is all there is to double entry bookkeeping. That does not mean that the whole thing is trivial. It is not. In a large firm, there will be large numbers of individual accounts, the balance of any one showing up as a tiny part of one side of the balance sheet. For any given transaction, it will take skill to know which two accounts should be updated, and it is trained accountants who give instructions in such matters, in former times to bookkeepers, but now, quite often to systems analysts designing computer systems.

We have not mentioned the equity portion of the liability side in terms of double-entry bookkeeping yet. There is an additional complexity there, which we shall come to presently. For now, let us just see how the simplest system would involve equity.

Suppose further that LSI sells $50,000 worth of chips one evening. This will increase the cash-on-hand portion of the balance sheet by $50,000, and also the equity portion by the same amount, as illustrated in Figure 2.5a and b. Again, two

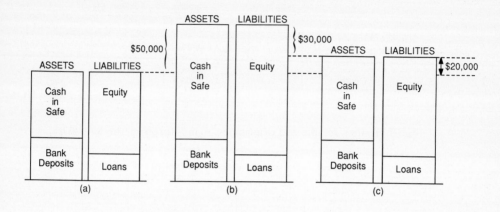

FIGURE 2.5.   How revenue and expenditures affect the balance sheet. In b we see how both the cash-on-hand (in the safe) and the equity increase by $50,000 when $50,000 worth of chips are sold. Later, when $30,000 worth of chips are redeemed (purchased), both cash on hand and equity fall by $30,000, as in c. However, the difference between revenue and expenditure here is $20,000, and we see that in c the final equity and cash-on-hand balances are $20,000 higher than in a, reflecting a gross income of $20,000.

entries are needed, with both sides of the balance sheet remaining equal, as always. Later that evening there are chip redemptions of $30,000. This means that the cash-on-hand will fall by $30,000 and the equity will fall by the same amount (Figure 2.5c). Again two entries are needed.

We can show the activities discussed above in the individual accounts behind the balance sheet:

ASSETS ACCOUNTS			EQUITY/LIABILITY ACCOUNTS		
Cash-on-hand			**Equity**		
TRANSACTION#	TYPE	AMOUNT	TRANSACTION#	TYPE	AMOUNT
(Prev. Balance	+	105,000)	(Prev. Balance	+	120,000)
2	+	40,000	3	+	50,000
3	+	50,000	4	−	30,000
4	−	30,000	[Curr. Balance	+	140,000]
[Curr. Balance	+	165,000]			

ASSETS ACCOUNTS	EQUITY/LIABILITY ACCOUNTS

LVFB demand deposit account

TRANSACTION#	TYPE	AMOUNT
(Prev. Balance	+	20,000)
[Curr. Balance	+	20,000]

Loan-1 from LVNB

TRANSACTION#	TYPE	AMOUNT
(Prev. Balance	+	30,000)
[Curr. Balance	+	30,000]

LNB demand deposit account

TRANSACTION#	TYPE	AMOUNT
(Prev. Balance	+	25,000)
1	+	40,000
2	–	40,000
[Curr. Balance	+	25,000]

Loan-1 from LNB

TRANSACTION#	TYPE	AMOUNT
(Prev. Balance	+	0)
1	+	40,000
[Curr. Balance	+	40,000]

Except for the previous and current balances, each entry in each account is referenced by a transaction number. Notice that each transaction number can be found in two accounts because of double-entry bookkeeping. The entries were taken (or posted) from the chronological sequence in the journal. Remember that the transactions we discussed are reflected in Figures 2.4 and 2.5 and were four in all:

Arrange a loan of $40,000 at LNB

Take $40,000 from LNB and place in safe

Sell $50,000 worth of chips

Redeem $30,000 worth of chips

These transactions are numbered in the journal:

JOURNAL:

TRANSACTION#	AMOUNT	EXPLANATION
1	$40,000	Borrowed from LNB, placed in LNB account
2	$40,000	Moved from account to safe
3	$50,000	Chip sales
4	$30,000	Chip redemption
. . .		

Each transaction is listed in the journal when it occurs. Later, at a convenient time, for each journal transaction, two entries are made in the individual accounts behind, or underlying, the balance sheet, as shown above. The accounts underlying the balance sheet are known as the general ledger accounts, and the process of taking an entry from the journal and making two entries in the general ledger is known as posting and is the fundamental bookkeeping operation.

If we look at the general ledger accounts above, we see that the previous balances lead us immediately to the balances sheet at the point in time just before the journal entries listed above. This initial balance sheet would be:

ASSETS		LIABILITIES	
Cash-on-hand	$105,000	Equity	$120,000
LVNB account	$20,000	Loan-1	$30,000
LNB account	$25,000	Balance:	$150,000
Balance:	$150,000		

As always, both sides match. After the series of transactions listed in the journal, the new balance sheet is obtained simply by adding (where there is a + sign), or subtracting (where there is a − sign), the amounts in each ledger account to get the current balances (actually shown at the bottom of each account). The current balance sheet will therefore be:

ASSETS		LIABILITIES	
Cash-on-hand	$165,000	Equity	$140,000
LVNB account	$20,000	Loan-1	$30,000
LNB account	$25,000	Loan-2	$40,000
Balance:	$210,000	Balance:	$210,000

And once more, the two sides balance.

No matter how many entries we make in the general ledger accounts, that is, accounts showing the increases and decreases over time of the quantities listed in the balance sheet, when we take the balances of each account and make up a balance sheet with them, the two sides will match—provided we have adhered to the rules of double-entry bookkeeping in posting journal entries to the ledger.

As we saw above, to check that everything is in balance, sum each ledger account to get the latest account balance, and then construct the latest balance sheet. In the case of LSI, which ledger accounts are from the asset side of the balance sheet and which are from the equity/liability side, is very obvious. In addition, we were careful to place asset accounts on the left side of the page and equity liability accounts on the right. However, in a large organization, there can be so many accounts that where they belong is not obvious, and the job of constructing a balance sheet is quite onerous. In particular, it is a job that you do not want to carry out without being sure beforehand that the two sides are going to match.

To check for a match without actually constructing the balance sheet from the ledger accounts, accountants invented the trial balance. The trial balance simply involves summations of the data in the ledger accounts. However, these is something that you have to think about to understand just what a trial balance entails.

Refer to Figure 2.4 again. If we have a ledger account liability entry to increase a loan by $40,000, then there will have to be an identical increase in one of the asset accounts as well, so that the two sides of the balance sheet still balance. That is one kind of ledger account entry: equal entries to accounts on both sides.

The other possibility is equal and opposite entries to accounts on one side. Consider the asset side in Figure 2.4. Suppose that $40,000 is taken from a demand deposit account and placed in the safe. Clearly the demand deposit account must have an entry showing a drop of $40,000, and the cash-on-hand account must have an entry showing an increase of $40,000. The total size of the asset column does not change. An increase in one part of the column is offset by a decrease elsewhere in the column.

These are essentially the only two types of entry we can have. Either we have equal amounts on both sides in the form of equal increases or equal decreases, or we have an increase and corresponding decrease on a single side. If we let A-account refer to an asset account, and L-account refer to an equity/liability account, then because the two sides of the balance sheet must always match, the following basic accounting equation is always true:

A-account increases − A-account decreases = L-account increases − L-account decreases

If total assets or total liabilities do not change, then:

A-account increases − A-account decreases = 0

or

L-account increases − L-account decreases = 0

Thus, if only one side is affected, the increase must equal the decrease, which we also saw in Figure 2.4b. If we are dealing only with increases then it also follows that:

A-account increases = L-account increases

which we also deduced from Figure 2.5b. It also follows from the accounting equation that:

A-account decreases = L-account decreases

when we are dealing only with decreases, which should also be obvious from Figure 2.4.

The Trial Balance

A trial balance simply involves summing all increases in the four categories—A-account increases, A-account decreases, L-account increases, L-account decreases—to see if they fit the accounting equation.

There is nothing more to a trial balance than that, except that accountants long ago introduced some addition jargon, which confuses all non-accountants. Look at the accounting equation again. If we rearrange things, we get:

A-account increases + L-account decreases
            = L-account increases + A-account decreases

Here is the special accounting jargon:

An A-account increase is called a debit
An L-account decrease is called a debit

An L-account increase is called a credit

An A-account decrease is called a credit

Thus, if we look at the rearrangement of the accounting equation again, we have:

A-account increase + L-account decrease = L-account increase + A-account decrease
(debit)   (debit)   (credit)   (credit)

If you know which entries are credits and which are debits, to do a trial balance, all you have to check is that the sum of the debits is the sum of the credits. Incidentally, do not think that something negative is associated with debit and something positive with credit. They are just accounting names.

As an example of this naming process for increases and decreases, depending on whether the account is A-type or L-type, we could rewrite the cash-on-hand account (an A-account) given earlier as:

Cash-on-hand

TRANSACTION#	TYPE	AMOUNT
Prev. Balance	+ (debit)	105,000
2	+ (debit)	40,000
3	+ (debit)	50,000
4	− (credit)	30,000

which shows that increases are debits with this type of account. On the other hand, we can rewrite the equity account given earlier as:

Equity

TRANSACTION#	TYPE	AMOUNT
Prev. Balance	+ (credit)	120,000
3	+ (credit)	50,000
4	− (debit)	30,000

which shows that increases are credits with this type of account.

The convention that A-account increases and L-account decreases are debits, and that L-account increases and A-account decreases are credits is very useful in practice, since in a complex firm with thousands of accounts, doing a trial balance will only involve checking that the sums of all credits and debits are equal for a given period.

It should be clear that the number of accounts required in the general ledger can multiply rapidly. Suppose that LSI kept cash in ten safes instead of just one. An account would be required for the increases and decreases if the cash in each safe, with a corresponding entry in the balance sheet for the balance in each safe. Suppose that LSI had twenty separate bank accounts. Twenty corresponding accounts would be needed in the ledger, and twenty corresponding balances for the balance sheet. Again, suppose that LSI had fifty different loans. An account would be needed for each loan (showing the initial increase when the funds were borrowed, and the decreases as the funds were paid back in steps).

Generally, the number of accounts can be kept small if the firm is small. However, there is one subdivision of accounts that is always undertaken, and this will be true even for a business as simple as LSI. The account that is always divided up is the equity account. There are many reasons for doing this, but probably the most important is the large volume of transactions that can require updating of the equity account. The transactions involved are revenues and expenditures.

Revenue and Expenditure Accounts

As we have seen, if LSI sells some chips, the resulting revenue is entered into a cash account on the asset side and the equity account on the liability side (Figure 2.5). There has to be an entry in the equity account, for if a firm gets some revenue, its assets grow, and since its debts do not change, the equity must grow. Similarly, if LSI redeems some chips (expenditures), a cash account on the asset side will decrease, and the equity will decrease.

The point is this. Increases in the equity account means revenues, and decreases mean expenditures. But the difference between revenue and expenditures is the firm's earnings or profit. Thus the balance of the entries into the equity account (excluding previous balance) is the firm's profit for the period.

The firm's profit shows up as an increase in the equity in the balance sheet (the difference between the equity listed in the balance sheet at the start of the period, and the equity listed in the balance sheet at the end of the period).

Because of the volume of revenue and expenditure entries, the equity account is broken up into two accounts, a revenue account and an expenditure account. Increases in the revenue account, like the equity account, must be credits, but increases in the expenditure account will have to be debits, if things are to work out. The division of the equity account into revenue and expenditure accounts is illustrated by the extended balance sheet in Figure 2.6a. If we just concentrate on the revenues and

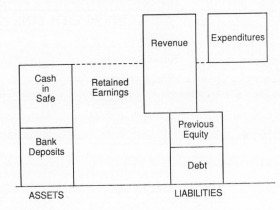

(a) Display of revenues and expenditures over time.

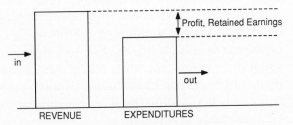

(b) Display of assets and liabilities (debt) over time.

FIGURE 2.6. Showing how revenue and expenditures, which actually form the income statement for a period as in (b), relate to the balance sheet, as in (a). Over a period of time, the difference between revenue and expenditure is added to the equity as retained earnings or profit.

expenditures, we have the two columns in Figure 2.6b. The one on the left (revenues) can be looked upon as a column of money coming into the firm, and the one on the right (expenditures) can be looked upon as a column of money leaving the firm. The difference is the firm's profit.

It is from the revenue and expenditure accounts that the firm's other important financial statement—the income statement—is generated. The income statement is very simple. It is merely the list of revenue and expenditure items over a period. It has subtotals by category and the difference between revenue and expenditures clearly stated. That is, the balance will appear in the balance sheet as the increase in equity. The income statement for LSI for a week could look like this:

INCOME STATEMENT, LSI, INC., WEEK ENDING 24TH JAN., 1988

REVENUES

Total chip sales	320,000

EXPENDITURES

Total chip redemptions	290,000
Heritage payment	2,000
Rent payment	20,000
Interest payment	800
Salary withdrawal	6,000
Total Expenditures	318,800
Net income	**1,2000**

The subdivision of the equity account into revenue and expenditure accounts normally does not stop at just two accounts. In practice, the expenditure account will be broken down into further smaller expenditure accounts, one for each category of expenditure. For example, a chip redemption account, a rental account, an interest account for each bank loan, and so on will be included. Similarly, the revenue account can be broken up into smaller revenue accounts, with one for each category of revenue.

Typically there are not nearly so many kinds of revenue accounts as expenditure accounts, for sources of revenue are normally scarce. LSI has only one category of revenue: chip sales. A large firm might have a revenue account for each product line in each region.

Computer System Design

With a firm grasp of accounting systems in general, and LSI's system in particular, Sarah Didjet now had to consider how the manual system could be replaced by a compute system. In its bare bones, the overall system required was quite clear. The different accounts would form a collection of computer files, or perhaps a data base, or data bases. There would also be a collection of programs to take care of updating and for generating reports, such as balance sheets, income statements, and so on. From listening to what Joe wanted, it was clear to Sarah that the system would have to be an online system. In other words, a person would go to the terminal and see a master menu. If you selected updating you would get a subsidiary menu listing types of updates you could have (for example, chip sales, rent, and so on). You would select one, such as rent, at which point the system would ask for the dollar figure involved.

Once a dollar figure was entered, the system would automatically enter this quantity in the journal, and into two general ledger accounts, in compliance with the rules for double-entry bookkeeping. The system would have the knowledge to tag an update to a general ledger account as a credit or debit. Later you could select trial balance as one of the options on the master menu. If the accounts did not balance, you would be able to have displays and printouts from any account, or from the journal entries. The data should be sufficiently cross-referenced to permit an accounting sleuth to trace the effect on the ledger accounts of an update to the journal.

That much was clear. Like all systems, this one boiled down to data structures and programs. The major question was whether to have files or data bases, although what programs were needed, in terms of program function, could be decided without knowledge of the exact structure of the data, Sarah could not do any detailed program design until the required data structures had been determined. She was up against one of the simplest, and yet most perplexing, data base design question. Sarah was quite perplexed, but decided that she had accomplished enough for one day and postponed thinking about the problem until the next day.

Files Versus Data Bases for LSI

Sarah was staying at the Lost Vegas Halltone Hotel. That was the hotel that housed LSI. Thus the hotel became her work place, except for the few hours she spent in the city library, which was only a ten minute walk away. At breakfast that morning, she began to concentrate once more on the LSI problem. There was one very simple solution. Use a standard accounting package. Such a package would let you make entries to a journal, set up ledger accounts, transfer or post journal entries to the ledger accounts, perform trial balances, and generate balance sheets and income statements. Such packages were eminently suited for small businesses. Why bother coming up with a custom solution for Joe's business?

Sarah gave this solution very serious consideration, but finally rejected it. The problem was Joe wanted to be able to use his data for all kinds of information retrieval and display that were not supported by such packages. Furthermore, such packages were designed to handle businesses with far more ledger accounts that Joe had. They could handle accounts receivable, accounts payable, fixed assets, depreciation, and other things that Joe had no need for. It would probably be cheaper to build a custom system for Joe than to modify some existing package, although the cost was probably not that important for a firm that made as much money as LSI. In the end it was the consideration that Joe would get a simpler and better system via the custom route that turned Sarah against the accounting package solution. That left her where she had been the previous evening—with the problem of files versus data bases.

She wondered if anyone had written up a description of a data base for the ledger accounts and journal of a business. She decided to check this out at the library at the local university (University of Lost Vegas). There she thumbed through the pages of about fifteen data base texts, but nowhere could she find an example of a data base for the ledger accounts of a firm. She could find examples involving one or two accounts from the ledger, such as accounts receivable, accounts payable, or fixed assets. She also noticed that many of the authors stated that a single comprehensive data base for all the important operational data of a firm was—to say the least—a dubious concept, and probably impractical.

All very well, thought Sarah, but what is wrong with a comprehensive corporate data base for a firm the size of Joe's, especially considering the size of Joe's income? At that moment, she made up her mind. Joe wants a data base for LSI, and he wants the best. Joe can afford and data base she cared to design. So a comprehensive data base for LSI is what Joe is going to have, even if we could do the job with just conventional files (and it looks as if we could).

The Proposed Data Base Design for LSI

That evening Sarah discussed the project on the telephone with her boss, Peter Stone, in San Fransisco. She explained her understanding of the problems, what Joe wanted, and how she thought that the best solution was a custom system with its own data base for journal and ledger data. She was relieved to find that Peter was very encouraging and felt that her thinking on the project was quite reasonable.

Before hanging up, he reminded her to make sure that Joe approved her screen designs before she came back to San Fransciso to work on the implementation. He added: "A system is no good if it doesn't do what the customer wants. The customer is always right. So make sure you get his approval for your screen designs in writing before you leave. I don't want any arguments after installation." Sarah made a note about that in red ink. In her eagerness to specify the system she had forgotten about written customer approval for the design—not the design of the data base, but the designs for the designs for what Joe would see on his screen, such as menus and displays.

In principle, the design for the journal was simple enough—a single conceptual file on disk, with tape backup for security. The design for the general ledger accounts required more thought. One possibility was a conceptual file for each general ledger account. As far as Sarah could see, there was nothing technically incorrect in such a collection of ledger conceptual files. But it seemed a messy solution. Instead she decided to go the other extreme and place all the general ledger accounts in a single conceptual file. This file, which she called LEDGER-POSTINGS, is illustrated in Figure 2.7. She called the conceptual file for the journal JOURNAL-ENTRIES.

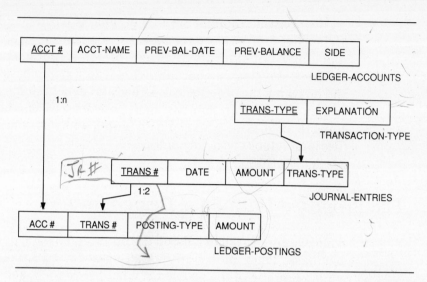

FIGURE 2.7.   Sarah Didget's design for the data base for all accounting data at LSI. The primary key fields are underlined. The data base could be implemented easily as either a CODASYL or relational data base. Because we are dealing with a network, use of a hierarchical data base management system, such as IBM's IMS, although possible, would be awkward. The major conceptual file in the data base is LEDGER-POSTINGS, which contains the entries for all the ledger accounts. In this conceptual file ACC# identifies the account involved, TRANS# identifies the journal entry (in JOURNAL-ENTRIES) from which the entry was posted, POSTING-TYPE indicates credit or debit entry, and AMOUNT gives the dollar amount involved. Notice that the relationship between JOURNAL-ENTRIES and LEDGER-POSTINGS is 1:2, because of the double-entry bookkeeping involved. A 1:2 relationship is a particular case of the common 1:n relationship.

To avoid redundancies and unwanted dependencies it would be more accurate to state that her computerized general ledger required two conceptual files, namely LEDGER-ACCOUNTS and LEDGER-POSTINGS, and that her computerized journal also required two conceptual files, namely TRANSACTION-TYPE and JOURNAL ENTRIES. All these conceptual files are illustrated, along with the relationships between them, in the extended Bachman diagram in Figure 2.7. In such diagrams primary key fields (or field combinations) are underlined, and arrows signify l:n relationships, and end on the foreign keys (or child connection fields) that suppost the relationships.

First let us examine the conceptual files TRANSACTION-TYPE and JOURNAL-ENTRIES that replace the manual journal. In JOURNAL-ENTRIES, the TRANS# field identifies a transaction by number, and records are entered in chronological order, which, in practice, means ascending TRANS# order. DATE gives the date of a transaction, and AMOUNT the dollar amount involved. TRANS-TYPE identifies the type of transaction, by means of a code. Different types of transactions could be (a) taking out a loan from Bank A, (b) paying rent, (c) selling chips, and so on. In the conceptual file TRANSACTION-TYPE the field EXPLANATION contains text explaning the type of transaction, along the lines of the explanations in the previous sentence. For a given type of transaction, there will be many records involving that type of transaction in JOURNAL-ENTRIES. Hence the l:n relationship between TRANSACTION-TYPE and JOURNAL-ENTRIES.

We next look at the conceptual files LEDGER-ACCOUNTS and LEDGER-POSTINGS that make up the general ledger. It is the conceptual file LEDGER-POSTINGS that contains the entries or jpostings to the general ledger. An entry is identified by the account number involved (ACC#) and the transaction number (TRANS#) of the journal transaction from which the entry was taken (or posted). POSTING-TYPE indicates a credit or debit entry. (How will this information be obtained, since it is not entered into the journal? Sarah has this figured out.) Amount gives the dollar amount involved.

The conceptual file LEDGER-ACCOUNTS gives more information about each account in the general ledger. ACC# identifies an account using a four digit account number. The first two digits identify the category of the account, and the next two the specific type of account. For example, all expenditure accounts could have 13 as the first two digits, so the 1301 could identify the rent account, 1302 the interest account on a certain loan, 1351, the taxes paid account, and so on. (In a large firm, 10 or 12 digits may be needed, to handle categories of accounts, subcategories, subcategories of subcategories, and so on.)

The field PREV-BAL in LEDGER-ACCOUNTS gives the balance of the account that was valid at the beginning of the period for which entries are recorded in the journal and postings in LEDGER-POSTINGS. In this way previous balances are kept separate from the increases and decreases in the accounts, as listed in LEDGER-POSTINGS. PREV-BALANCE-DATE gives the date on which this balance applied, which will also be the date at which entries into the journal began.

When new balances of all accounts are obtained at the end of a prescribed accounting period, typically three months, these latest balances will be stored in LEDGER-ACCOUNTS, replacing the old balances, and the data in both JOURNAL-ENTRIES and LEDGER-POSTINGS deleted, but not before being transferred to archival versions of the two files. Following updating of LEDGER-ACCOUNTS with new balances, JOURNAL-ENTRIES and LEDGER-POSTIONGS can then fill up again over the following three months. The field SIDE in LEDGER-ACCOUNTS indicates the side of the balance sheet to which an account properly belongs. For example a loan account belongs on the equity/liability side, and a cash account belongs on the asset side.

Operation of the System

On a daily basis, the operator at a terminal has to enter transactions as they occur. The system then updates the journal and carries out posting to two accounts covered in LEDGER-POSTINGS, that is, double-entry bookkeeping.

In more detail, to receive a new journal transaction, the system displays the contents of TRANSACTION-TYPE on the operator's display screen, requesting that the operator select the type of transaction. It then asks for the amount involved. Having accepted this, it assigns the next number in sequence to the TRANS# field, assigns the date to DATE, places the dollar amount in AMOUNT, and the transaction type code in TRANS-TYPE. It then stores the newly constructed record in JOURNAL-ENTRIES.

The next step for the system is to post this journal entry to the ledger. Two records will have to be placed in LEDGER-POSTINGS; the ACC# field value will be different in these two records. How does the system know which two accounts need to have entries? It keeps a separate action control file equating transaction type code (number) with the two accounts that need updating. Sarah has called this file POSTING-CONTROL, and a record is shown below:

TRANS-TYPE	ACC-1	TYPE-1	ACC-2	TYPE-2
T22	3514	'DEBIT'	5418	'CREDIT'

This record says that if you have a journal transaction of type T22, then the amount involved will be used to debit account 3514, and credit account 5418. Thus to determine what updating action is needed following an entry in the journal file JOUR-NAL-ENTRIES, the system looks up the transaction type in POSTING-CONTROL to determine which accounts in the ledger need entries, and whether an entry should be marked credit or debit. [POSTING-CONTROL records could be concatenated to TRANSACTION-TYPE records in the data base, as another alternative; see Question 7.] If the operator at the terminal wanted a trial balance, the system would simply sum all the credits and debits in LEDGER-POSTINGS separately, and display the two sums. If they do not match, the system can help find the reason, by permitting display of the records in both JOURNAL-ENTRIES, using TRANS#, ACC#, TRANS-TYPE, and DATE to identify either a record or group of records for display, and in LEDGER-POSTINGS.

If the operator requests a balance sheet (by selecting the balance sheet option from the master menu), the system will sum the debits and credits for all asset side accounts (it knows which accounts are asset side from information in LEDGER-ACCOUNTS). The balance of each account will be added to (if a debit), or subtracted from (if a credit), the previous account balance stored in LEDGER-ACCOUNTS. Equity/liability accounts are treated similarly, except that credit balances are added to previous balances in LEDGER-ACCOUNTS, and debit balances are subtracted. (An exception is made in the case of expense accounts, where, if you have followed the material on LSI's accounting system, you will understand that debit balances are added to, and not subtracted from, the corresponding expense account previous balances stored in LEDGER-ACCOUNTS.) Once all the new current balances are available for LEDGER-ACCOUNTS, the displayed (or printed) balance sheet is essentially the ACC-NAME and PREV-BALANCE values from LEDGER-ACCOUNTS, with one small amount of additional processing. The balances in revenue and expense accounts are not displayed directly. Instead, the difference between revenue balance and total expense account balances is displayed as the balance of retained earnings (equity). See Figure 2.6 for further clarification of this.

To have the income statement displayed, the system displays the balance of the revenue account, and the balance of each expense account, together with profit (earnings, or retained earnings) displayed as the difference between the revenue balance and the sum of the expense account balances. The balances involved can be for any arbitrary period, such as a week or ten days, although there will be a specific requirement for the income statement over a period of three months. But see also question 8.

Balance sheets for each of a sequence of points of time, for example, every 7 days, can also be obtained, using the method described above for each balance sheet generation. From this sequence of balance sheets, a plot of any account balance or sum of account balances (such as total assets, total debt, and so on) can be displayed.

Income statements for consecutive periods of time can also be generated, using the method described above for each income statement. The period could be a day, a few days, a week, and so on. From this sequence of income statements, a plot of any expense account balance, or sum of such balances (for example, total revenue, total expenses, total interest payments) can be displayed.

In addition to this, Sarah decided to open up the possibility for ad hoc queries to the data base, using an SQL-based relational data base system. Thus queries like:

Sum all credits to account 1487.

can be expressed using SQL as follows:

```
SELECT SUM(AMOUNT)
FROM LEDGER-POSTINGS
WHERE POSTING-TYPE = 'CREDIT' AND ACC# = '1487';
```

Computer System

Sarah considered placing the whole thing on a personal computer, such as an IBM PC/XT or AT (both with sealed hard disks and capacity exceeding 10 MB). This seemed reasonable, since it looked as if only one operator would ever use the system at any one time. Instead of tape drive back up, removable floppy disks would hold the back up (and archived) data. She discussed this with Joe. But Joe would not have it. (His anti-complexity instinct did not fail him.) "The only thing that's going to spin in this establishment is my roulette wheel", he said. "There's no way you're going to get me to push floppy disks in and out." So Sarah decided to use a local service bureau running IBM's SQL-based data base system DATABASE2, with a terminal on Lucy's desk. Joe thought that that was more like what he had in mind.

Postscript

Before she returned to San Francisco, Sarah got Joe's written agreement about the format of the screen displays that the system would use and about the effects of option selections. He also agreed that the CONTROL-POSTINGS file would limit the types of transactions to those available at installation; new types of transactions could be accommodated only if service personnel from Cybertek made appropriate entries in CONTROL-POSTINGS.

Back at Cybertek's main office, Sarah detailed the specifications for each module of the system and for associated data bases. Peter Stone approved the design (but not before long discussions and suggestions for minor improvements, which we will not go into). Peter then put three programmers to work construction the modules, and seven weeks later the system was functioning at LSI in Lost Vegas.

It is true that Sarah's system is a fairly expensive system, but Joe never misses the money. In fact, it probably saves him money, because he now knows the state of his finances every day and has been able to reduce the amount of debt at the banks, most of which he had never really needed but had kept outstanding just in case.

At any rate, both Joe's salary and LSI's profits have continued to grow since the system was installed. And as you might expect, Joe just pays a fixed monthly sum to Cybertek, and this covers everything. (There is an account for this in LEDGER-ACCOUNTS.) It is Cybertek who deals with the computer service bureau in Lost Vegas—not Joe. Even with his sophisticated computer system, on a foundation of IBM's flagship relational data base system, Joe continues to keep things simple. As Joe is fond of saying, making money should be as easy as adding two and two and getting five.

Questions

1. Prepare a detailed listing of the programs or modules that will be used with the Cybertek data base in Figure 2.7. For each program or module, give a brief description of the logic, particularly with regard to how the data base is accessed or updated.

2. Given an entirely different design for the data base in Figure 2.7, with a conceptual file for each account of the general ledger instead. Compare your design with that in Figure 2.7, by (a) listing the major differences in the way the data base would be accessed and updated, and (b) giving advantages and disadvantages of both designs. Do not assume that the design in Figure 2.7 is the best design; your design may be superior.

3. In the core relation LEDGER-POSTINGS in Figure 2.7, AMOUNT is functionally dependent on TRANS#, which is a subkey field and not a primary field. Confirm this. In theory, that is bad. However, in this specific case it does no harm, in the case writer's opinion. Discuss this. You could eliminate the dependency just by removing the AMOUNT field from LEDGER-POSTINGS. Confirm this. Would such elimination be an improvement? Discuss this too.

4. If a record is placed in LEDGER-POSTINGS, typically an additional record must also be entered, to comply with the requirements of double-entry bookkeeping. This means

that the conceptual file contains some kind of dependency. Discuss this. Is it dangerous? Discuss the possibility of getting rid of this dependency.

5. In question 2 above, you were asked to come up with a design where each general ledger account was implemented as a separate conceptual file. What kind of dependency, if any, is introduced by the requirements of double-entry bookkeeping. Discuss this.

6. Discuss the whole issue of data bases to permit the equivalent of double-entry bookkeeping. Are we just allowing some convention from the past, which was understandable in as area of manual bookkeeping, to clutter up our elegant theory of 4NF/5NF data base design? Discuss this.

7. Redesign the conceptual file TRANSACTION-TYPE to include the data in the hidden control file POSTING-CONTROL. How would doing this affect things in practice?

8. As the data base in Figure 2.7 is designed, there is no information about dates in the ledger files, so how do we actually get an income statement for any given period? Outline the algorithm. Is there any reason to change the data base design because of this?

THREE

Silicon Mountain Supplies, Inc.

Silicon Mountain Supplies (SMS) is a wholesaler of silicon integrated circuits (ICs), the kind that are commonly found in all modern electronic equipment, especially computers. An integrated circuit contains a silicon chip, enclosed in a package. The chip is a square slice of silicon, metallic in appearance, about the size of the nail of your small finger. One surface of such a chip has been heavily processed, by fine chemical methods, to generate an interconnected complex of many thousands of miniaturized transistors.

Chips can be made for a few dollars each, or even less, despite their complexity. They are manufactured in large batches of a hundred or more circular wafers of processed silicon, each wafer (like a silicon "cookie") about three inches in diameter and containing many chips. Following chemical formation of the circuit chips on the circular wafers, each wafer is sliced to give the individual chips.

The final stage of manufacturing is the wiring (or wire-bonding) of the chip into a plastic, metal, or ceramic package. A package can be quite big compared with the size of the enclosed silicon chip. For example, a package about two inches by a half inch is not uncommon. A packaged circuit will have an array of interconnection pins along two sides to enable the circuit to be inserted into an electronic circuit board.

It is the packaged integrated circuits that SMS deals in. SMS never touches the manufacturing end of IC production. That requires hundreds of millions of dollars in capital for just a minimal production setup. SMS buys ICs in large quantities from manufacturers, warehouses them, and sells them, usually in smaller batches, to manufacturers of computers and other electronic equipment.

You might ask why the electronics firms do not buy their ICs direct from the manufacturer. The answer is that they usually do. However, often they cannot get the quantity needed exactly when they want it. The chip manufacturers' primary working parameter is the chip yield—that is, the percentage of working chips that they can get out of slicing a silicon wafer. But the production process is sensitive to chemical contamination, which can cause the yield to vary widely over time for any given line of chips at any given plant. Thus a customer can find that because of current low production yields, a supplier cannot fill an order for many months in the future. This is where SMS comes in. SMS buys carefully, especially when suppliers are high and prices are low, but always with an eye to advancing technology.

When electronics manufacturers cannot get supplied by a manufacturer they turn to companies like SMS. SMS, and firms like it, are not what you would call popular among the manufacturers, who tend to regard them as something akin to parasites, especially when such IC wholesalers sell imported ICs. Firms like SMS respond that they are simply filling a market need, and that they prefer to buy American product, when they can get it at acceptable price and quality.

Despite the bad feeling that tends to exist between IC manufacturers and this type of wholesaler, SMS is generally well regarded in manufacturing circles. SMS buys only the highest quality and is certainly no fly-by-night operator that just skims the cream. The firm was started in the 1974 recession by Tom Sayles. Tom had been marketing manager at Silectronics, one of the big chip manufacturers in California's Silicon Valley. Silectronics had borrowed heavily in the golden years of 1972 and 1973 to finance development and construction of state-of-the-art IC production facilities. Silectronics management had expected that sales of new product would more than pay for the loans they had incurred. It did not work that way. The 1974 recession struck with a vengeance, markets turned soft, and prices plunged, taking Silectronics into bankruptcy, and giving Tom Sayles a lesson he never forgot.

For a brief spell in 1974 Tom had been unemployed, unable to find any work in marketing. He had some savings and a house with a double garage. In the time-honored tradition of the valley, SMS was started in Tom's garage. Tom had been through some of the ups and down of the semiconductor industry before, but never anything as bad as the 1974 recession. Having watched companies chasing the market on a day-to-day basis for years, Tom came to the conclusion that there was money to be made by a firm that bought high quality product with long term viability at low prices at times when nobody wanted it, and sold it again at high prices when the market was clammoring for product. He swore that he would never repeat the mistake of Silectronics management, who had bought product manufacturing capacity at high prices in boom times, going heavily into debt to do so, only to have to sell the resulting product at very low recession prices.

SMC is located in San Jose, not far from most of the Silicon Valley chip manufacturers. The premises are rented, furniture and all. Most of the space is warehouse space for storage of the integrated circuits. The building is equipped with humidifiers to eliminate static electricity, which is a menace to integrated circuits. There are only two employees, Fred Store who looks after the warehouse and Joan Wright who looks after the office. At the front of the building is Joan's office (Figure 3.1), located near the main entrance, so that Joan also doubles as receptionist. Next to Joan's office is a small conference room, used for sales presentations, and next to that is Tom's modestly furnished office.

There is a loading/unloading ramp for the warehouse, and Fred has a small office just adjacent to the ramp. The integrated circuits are usually in cardboard boxes, of varying sizes, on rows of shelves in the warehouse storage area. Everything in on one floor, as shown in Figure 3.1.

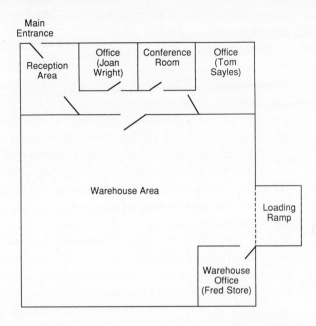

FIGURE 3.1. The building that houses Silicon Mountain Supplies Inc. (SMS).

Business Activities at SMS

Business at SMC is very simple in principle. Tom buys IC's at one price and sells them at another price. However, it requires special skill to know what and when to buy. An amateur might buy high quality ICs at low prices only to discover later they they had become obsolete and unsalable. Tom rarely makes such as mistake, although he expects it to happen once in a while. To avoid making a fatal mistake, however, Tom never puts a lot of his capital into any one purchase. Thus, if a deal does go sour, only a small fraction of his working capital is lost.

Tom spends most of his day on the telephone, talking to marketing managers at the IC manufacturers, purchasing managers at electronic equipment manufacturers, and his other important contacts throughout the industry. This keeps him on top of trends in the business.

Before placing an order to buy ICs, Tom will have carried out extensive negotiations with the marketing people at the IC manufacturer. When details of price, quantity, quality, reliability, delivery, and price have been worked out, Tom hands the process of issuing a purchase requisition over to Joan Wright. The supplier of the parts looks after delivery. On arrival the parts are given a careful visual inspection by Fred Store. If there is a problem, Fred reports to Joan, who notifies the supplier of refusal to accept the goods. SMS has no electronic test equipment and so has no way of checking that the quality or reliability of the parts received meet the purchase specifications. Tom has to trust the suppliers. However, they all know that if they ship him junk, Tom will never deal with them again, and they need his business. It is known that there are firms that Tom will not deal with for this very reason. It is only by such as ruthless approach that SMS can keep it reputation for quality at low cost.

Similarly, before an equipment manufacturer places an order with Tom for parts, extensive negotiations take place on the telephone. The purchase requisition, which usually arrives by mail, is handled by Joan Wright. Tom does not pay for shipment. He does not want responsibility for the parts once they leave SMS. The purchaser is required to provide and pay for shipment. This also helps Tom maintain quality. Furthermore, it simplifies his business.

Both purchases and sales are on credit. Thus, at any one time, there is a list of suppliers who have shipped Tom parts, but have not yet been paid. These unpaid bills are called accounts payable. Similarly, there will be a list of customers, to whom SMS has shipped parts, but from whom payment has not yet been obtained. These bills are called accounts receivable. For any given supplier listed in accounts payable, there may be one or more shipments on which payment in full has yet to be made by SMS. Similarly, for any given purchaser listed in accounts receivable, there may be one ore more shipments on which payment in full has yet to be remitted.

Tom manages his cash very carefully, and never pays a bill before he has to. Funds are kept in an account at the Federal

State Bank of California (FSBC). Mindful of the experience of his former employer, Silectronics, SMS has no debt, apart from accounts payable. The balance sheet is thus fairly simple, the example in Figure 3.2 being typical. At any given instant, the assets of the firm comprise its cash at FSBC, its accounts receivable, and the value of the inventory (at cost). The accounts receivable count as an asset, since these are funds to be received in a short time. The liability side consists of the debt implicit in the accounts payable, and the equity.

It should be clear that SMS, despite its small size, is in a very strong financial position. If disaster were to strike, rendering total inventory and all accounts receivable worthless but requiring that Tom still pay his accounts payable, the remaining equity in the firm would still be $50,000. Make sure you see this. Tom always makes sure that his cash is at least twice accounts payable, so that bankruptcy would be inconceivable for SMS, even in the worst of times.

On the revenue/expenditure side of things, the firm is also quite simple. Each month the firm pays out about $50,000 for

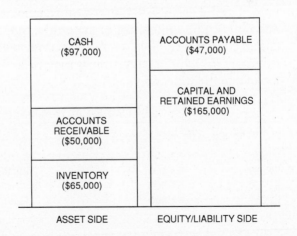

FIGURE 3.2. Typical balance sheet at SMS. Notice that the firm is in a very strong position financially. If the bottom were to drop out of the IC market, so that accounts receivable and inventory assets became worthless, SMS would still be able to pay its creditors (the suppliers) the $47,000 owed in accounts payable, leaving $50,000 in equity for the owner of the firm on liquidation.

parts, and takes in about $70,000. Other revenue is about $1,000 per month in interest. Other expenditures are $4,000 per month, telephone at $1,000 per month, electric utilities at $500 per month, and office expenditures at $500 per month. This leaves a net of about $10,000 per month, of which about $6,000 per month is paid out to Tom as a salary. The net profit of about $4,000 stays in the firm as part of equity.

Tom's salary is paid directly to an accountant, who looks after all deductions, including a fee for accounting services. Tom's net pay is about $4,000 per month, although it is the $6,000 monthly gross figure that appears in the firm's accounts.

SMS's Documentation System

Before studying the SMS system of keeping accounts and other information, readers are asked to be familiar with the concepts of accounting journal, general ledger accounting, posting with double-entry bookkeeping, and generation of balance sheet and income statement from the general ledger accounts. These matters were explained in Chapter 2.

The main general ledger accounts kept by SMS are as follows. On the asset side there is one cash account, an inventory account, and a collection of accounts, one for each customer, called accounts receivable. Each customer has an identification number, and for a given customer, the receivables account looks like the following:

CUSTOMER C44 receivables

INVOICE#	RECEIVABLE	D/C	DATE	COMMENT
INV56	$2,300	D	22/08/87	BILL
INV58	$3,100	D	29/08/87	BILL
INV56	$1,000	C	30/08/87	REMITTANCE
INV59	$1,000	D	02/09/87	BILL

A line in the account gives the invoice number for a shipment of parts sent to the customer, and either the funds originally owed on that invoice (a debit entry in the D/C column) or funds remitted by the customer in payment (in whole or in part) for that invoice (a credit entry). If we sum under the column RECEIVABLE (remembering that credits are negative in this case), we get the total owed by a customer. In the case of customer C44 above, this figure is $5,400. If we sum for the receivable balances of all the customers, we get the figure for the total accounts receivable for the firm, a figure which could appear in the balance sheet for that point in time.

On the equity/liability side we have the accounts payable and the equity accounts. There is an account payable for each supplier. Each supplier has an identification number, and the payables account for a given supplier looks like the following:

Supplier S33 payables

INVOICE#	PAYABLE	D/C	DATE	COMMENT
INV42	$1,500	C	02/12/1987	BILL
INV42	$1,200	D	09/12/1987	REMITTANCE
INV43	$2,500	C	14/12/1987	BILL
INV47	$2,000	C	21/12/1987	BILL

Each line in the account gives the invoice number for a parts shipment from the supplier, and either the amount originally owed to the supplier on that invoice or funds remitted to the supplier in payment for an invoice. If we sum the PAYABLE column for a supplier we get the total amount owed that supplier, and if we sum for all payables accounts we get the total amount owed suppliers by SMS at that point in time—that is, the total accounts payable, which could appear in the balance sheet for that point in time.

The equity account is divided into revenue and expenditure accounts. There are only two revenue accounts, one for revenue due to IC sales and the other for revenue from interest received from the bank. There is an expenditure account for each type of expenditure, such as expenditures on ICs, rent, telephone, and so on. Remember (Chapter 2) that according to conventional accounting practice, the balance of a revenue account is a credit and the balance of an expenditure account is a debit. The balance of accounts payable is, of course, a credit, since it is an account corresponding to the equity/liability side of the balance sheet.

Now let us see how these accounts function. Suppose that SMS buys $1,000 worth of ICs from supplier S33. The goods are shipped to SMS with an invoice requesting payment. On receipt of the invoice and a packing slip from Fred, Joan enters the $1,000 for the ICs in the journal. (The packing slip arrives with the goods, and lists the contents; Fred confirms that the physical shipment matches the packing slip list.)

Joan then uses the journal entry to post the information to the general ledger. She must update the inventory account by $1,000, since the firm's assets have clearly increased by that amount (a debit entry). The cash account is not affected, since SMS has not paid for these goods and it not intending to pay for them for some time. Instead, the account payable for supplier S33 gets an entry for $1,000 (a credit entry). Some time later, SMS makes a payment of $1,000 against that particular invoice. This payment is first recorded in the journal, and later, in posting to the general ledger, Joan places a $1,000 credit entry in the cash account and a $1,000 debit entry (for a remittance) in the accounts payable for S33.

We have drawn a diagram of what happens to the balance sheet during this process of receiving goods from a supplier (Figure 3.3). The diagram shows how the purchase first affects

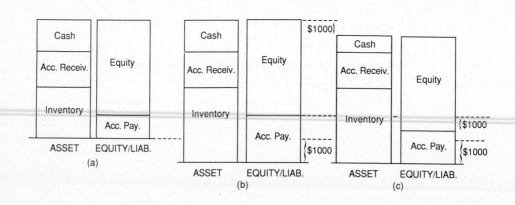

FIGURE 3.3. Showing how the purchase of $1,000 worth of components affect the balance sheet, when the purchase is first made with credit, and only later paid for in cash. In (a) we have the situation before receipt of the goods. In (b) we show the situation immediately after receipt of the goods. Both the inventory and the accounts payable have increased by $1,000. Total assets have also increased, matched by an increase in equity/liability; however, equity is unchanged. In (c) we show the situation after the debt has been paid by $1,000 cash from the firm's cash. Cash falls by $1,000, matched by a fall in accounts payable. Assets are now what they were originally.

inventory and accounts payable, and later how paying for the goods affects cash and accounts payable.

Notice that no expenditure account is affected by such as purchase. This is very important. The purchase of the parts does not become an expense until the goods are sold, since the parts, prior to sale, are physically in the firm, keeping up the value of the firm's inventory. Presently we shall look at exactly how the sale of the parts to a customer affects expenditure accounts, but first we must look at the inventory account.

We mentioned above that when the parts are received, Joan updates the inventory account. This account is also used for keeping track of what part types are in the warehouse. The account looks like this:

PART-TYPE NUMBER	SUPPLIER	INVOICE	QUANTITY	COST	DATE
7440	S67	INV13	+1,000	+2,500	02/11/87
7440	S67	INV15	+500	+1,500	25/12/87
7440	S42	INV56	+500	+1,000	03/12/87
7480	S45	INV99	+1,000	+2,000	05/12/87
7440	S67	INV13	−500	−1,250	01/01/88

Part types are segregated by the invoice under which they were received and by supplier. This should be clear from the first entries for part type 7440. Prices (per unit) change all the time, and so the parts invoiced on 02/11/87 cost $2,500/1000 or $2.50 per unit; a little while later, on the 25th of the same month, a new batch of 500 of the same part type cost $3.00 per unit.

With the above account, at any given time, Joan can say what part types are in the warehouse, what the supplier is, and the cost of each batch of any kind of part. What happens if Joan sells some parts? Suppose that she sells 500 of the 7440 ICs that were invoiced in INV13, and which cost SMS $2.50 per unit. An entry of the reduction of inventory is made for this part type (last entry above). The entry shows minus 500 for the part type quantity, shows the supplier and invoice involved, and gives a figure of minus $1,200 for the reduction in the value of the inventory. The major point is this. When parts are received, the inventory account is debited by the cost of the parts; later, when some of those same parts are sold, the inventory account is credited by the cost figure arrived at by multiplying the number of parts sold by the unit cost figure.

With this account for inventory, the sum of debits plus credits will give the total value (at cost) of the inventory at the particular point in time. This figure can be used for generating the balance sheet.

Now let us look at the mechanism of selling parts. Suppose that Joan sells a quantity of 500 of 7440 parts to customer C12, from whom a purchase order has been received. Parts are not shipped from SMS without a purchase order. Joan prepares a packing slip (bill of lading) describing the parts shipped; this she forwards to Fred Store, who packages the parts, together with a copy of the packing slip, ready for shipment. The customer's freight service picks them up at the warehouse. Then Joan prepares an invoice, a copy of which is mailed to the customer.

The 500 parts of type 7440 are sold for $2,000, that is, for $4.00 each. The parts sold are those that were originally purchased on invoice INV13 at $2.50 per unit. It is important to understand that to post the journal entry for the $2,000 to the general ledger, four entries are needed, because in reality two events must be recorded. These events are (a) 500 parts are removed from inventory (cost value $1,250), and (b) 500 parts are shipped to a customer in return for $2,000. This is tricky, but we are at the heart of the accounting process for recording the generation of profits in a business that buys and sells on credit. For each of two implicit transactions, double-entry bookkeeping requires two entries to the ledger, giving four entries in all.

First Joan deals with the reduction in inventory. An entry for minus $1,250 is made in the inventory account (as was shown above, last line of account). There is a corresponding entry in an expense account, the account for expenses in buying parts, showing an expense of $1,250 (a debit). Refer to Figure 3.4b for clarification. This debit to the expense account is really a mechanism for reducing equity to cover loss of inventory. Note that it is only at this point, when the goods leave SMS, that the expense of purchasing them is recorded as an expense.

Next Joan deals with the actual sale (Figure 3.4c). The goods are sold on credit, so that an entry for $2,000 is made in the receivables account for customer C12. This is a debit entry. A corresponding credit entry is made in the revenue account for sale of ICs, again an entry of $2,000. This entry really is just an increase in equity to match the increase in receivables.

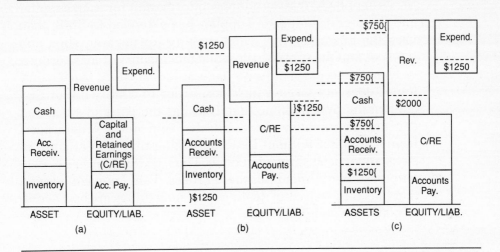

FIGURE 3.4.   Showing how the initial balance sheet in (a) is affected by the sale, for $2000, of parts originally purchased for $1250. First, as shown in (b), E, inventory is reduced by $1250, and thus also equity, in the form of an increase in expenditures by $1250. Expenditure increases, not when parts are bought for inventory, but when those parts are finally moved out of inventory and sold. Finally, as shown in (c) accounts receivable is increased by $1250 + $750, or $2000, balanced by an increase in equity, in the form of an increase in revenue, equal to $2000. Because of the increase in expenditures (in (b)) by $1250, the $2000 increase in revenue gives a net increase in equity (revenue minus expenditures) of $2000 - $1250, or $750, which is the profit on the deal. As a result, both asset and equity/liability columns in (c) are each $750 larger than in (a).

As a result of these four ledger entries, inventory has decreased by $1,250, accounts receivable has increased by $2,000, sales revenue has increased by $2,000, and expenditures have increased by $1,250. The debits and credits obviously match, so that the underlying balance sheet remains balanced. In addition, the difference between revenue and expenditure is $2,000—$1,250 or $750, which is the net increase in the equity, or additional retained earnings, or profit on the deal. All this is displayed by the diagrams in Figure 3.4.

In addition to the accounts required by the accounting system, two other files are necessary for conducting the business. One is a file that describes the firm's customers, with information about each customer's address and the limit of credit that will be extended by SMS. The other is a file that describes the firm's suppliers; it gives address information for each supplier and the credit limit each supplier has extended to SMS. Joan uses the customer file when making up packing slips and invoices and the supplier file when making up purchase orders.

There is no problem with back orders at SMS, since a customer does not issue a purchase order to SMS without first confirming by telephone that Tom has the parts in stock and can deliver immediately. Similarly, Tom never orders parts from a supplier without first confirming that the parts are in stock and can be shipped at once. Thus, SMS never has to deal with partially fulfilled purchase orders. Tom long ago learned that the complexities of dealing with such things are best avoided—and not computerized.

Introduction to Data Base Management at SMS, Inc.

Although Tom Sayle's business is clearly successful and quite profitable, it's management is a hectic affair for Tom. A particularly difficult problem is not accepting orders for which there are no parts in stock. Suppose that there were 1,000 ICs of type 3333 in stock from two distinct invoices. Suppose now that a customer phoned asking for 700 of these parts. Tom would immediately check with Joan about how many 3333's were in stock. If 700 out of the 1,000 in stock were from the same supplier, Tom would tell the customer to go ahead and submit the order. Otherwise the supplier would have to order part (say 300) made by one supplier and the rest (400) from the other supplier, all of which has to be explained to the customer. Joan would keep a note of this expected order in a manual Orders Expected file.

Suppose now, that a few days later a second customer asks for 600 of type 3333 ICs. The first customer has not yet submitted an order for the 700 parts, so that there are still 1,000 of the 3333's in stock. As usual, Tom asks Joan about how many parts are in stock. Joan checks the inventory account and obtains the number 1,000, but also checks the Orders Expected file, and informs Tom that SMS is also expecting an order for 700 from the first customer. Thus there are not enough 3333 parts in stock, and the order has to be refused.

Tom then starts phoning a number of suppliers to see what

kind of price he will have to pay for a new supply of 3333 devices. If he judges the price too high, he will simply not order. (Remember Tom buys parts when nobody wants them, and sells them when customers are beating the doors down.) When Tom does ask Joan to issue a purchase order for parts, she makes a note of this in a Parts-on-Order file.

All this is very time consuming, and Joan is more than busy, issuing purchase orders, invoices, packing slips, retrieving information for Tom, and keeping the books. Although he likes to keep things simple and has little respect for computers, Tom is slowly coming to the conclusion that a computer system for routine chores would be a great help. In this mind's eye he visualizes just checking a video display screen in front of him when a customer calls, so that he can get the complete picture for any individual type of part—how many are in stock, what they cost, how many are committed to orders not yet received, how many are on order, and so on. Tom figures that the computer system might just allow him, in certain instances, to accept orders from customers for parts that are not in stock but are on order. With only a manual system Tom feels that accepting such orders is far too risky.

An additional benefit or a computer system would be instant up-to-date displays of sales trends in any type of IC, as well as trends in prices paid and prices obtained. This would help Tom make better purchasing decisions and better pricing decisions on sales. The sales trends versus quantity in stock would also give him a better control on when and what to reorder. (Tom will not have automatic reorder in any type of part. The nature of his business does not allow it. A human decision must be made with each purchase order, involving, as we have seen, telephone calls to many suppliers. A technical part of the IC business, which is relevant here, is that any widely used part type has a standard electronic function and will be made by a large number of suppliers. Such parts from different suppliers are interchangeable as far as use in electronic equipment is concerned, although quality and reliability will vary. Thus, when an IC type from one supplier is depleted in Tom's warehouse, he might replace it with the same part type from a different manufacturer because of a purchase price/quality advantage. So automatic reorder is not possible for SMS.)

Tom has heard of a reputable firm, with which readers of the previous chapter should be familiar, called Cybertek International, Inc., of San Francisco. This firm's reputation for design-ing and installing data base systems for businesses large and small has impressed Tom. So one day, Tom drives up to Cybertek's San Francisco office, following a brief but promis-ing telephone conversation with Peter Stone, Cybertek's vice president in charge of customer systems development.

Computer System Design

At Cybertek, Tom explains his business to Peter Stone. Tom overdoes the details a bit, especially with regards to ICs, but Peter understands enough to see that although Tom's business is not all that complicated, it does have certain unique complex-ities (as does any business). It is also clear to him that Tom cannot afford a luxury system, but would be greatly helped by a basic system, possibly running on an advanced PC with multi-ple terminals. Peter agrees with Tom that a data base, or possi-bly two data bases, could be used for the routine operational and accounting data of the firm. Such data bases, with an associated manipulation system, would relieve Joan of an increasingly intolerable burden and, at the same time, provide Tom with information for making tactical decisions.

Toward the end of the meeting, Peter proposes a seven-to-ten week design and development period, outlines the approximate cost, and promises to send an analyst down to SMS very soon to observe the operation of the business first hand. Tom agrees to this and returns to San Jose, wondering why, after so many years selling ICs for use in computers, he has never made any use of computer to help his business operations.

After Tom Sayles left Cybertek's offices, Peter Stone went upstairs to discuss the new project with Joan Brayns, Cybertek's president and founder. Although the project was a relatively small one, on hearing about it Joan expressed the opinion that it was an important project for SMS because of the standing of Tom Sayles in Silicon Valley.

"Tom is widely known and respected by both the manufac-turers of integrated circuits and the equipment manufacturers who use those integrated circuits," she mused. "If we do a poor job for him or charge him far too much", she went on, "it'll be all over the valley quicker than you can say random access memory."

Joan through for a while. Finally she said: "Let's send Sarah Didjet to design the system. She did a good job up at Lucky Strike in Los Vegas. I've called Joe Sharp several times to find out how he likes the system Sarah designed. He's very happy with it. This project is similar, although the management of inventory, accounts, receivable, and accounts payable add additional complexity. I'm sure Sarah can handle it—with a little help from her friends here at Cybertek. This project will also help Sarah's development, and we may as well kill two birds with one stone. If we do a good job, we may get some major projects with those large IC manufacturing firms in the area. Let's give it our best effort. Put Sarah on it as once."

Next morning, after a briefing from Peter Stone, Sarah Didjet was on her way down the expressway to San Jose and SMS. Sarah lived near Stanford, between San Francisco and San Jose, so that a project with a San Jose firm was very convenient for her. It meant that she could drive either to SMS or to her Cybertek office, as required, without any need to stay in hotels, something she preferred to avoid.

As she pulled into the parking lot at SMS, she noticed that the property was pleasantly landscaped, with grass, bushes, some trees, and even some flowers. She has been in business long enough to have observed that well-run firms usually look well on the outside. Then she wondered who looked after the landscaping. There had been no mention of landscaping services. Later she found out that Fred Stone, who looked after the warehouse, was also part time gardener. There has to be an account for gardening costs, she thought.

She spent the day talking to Joan Wright, trying to make sense of the accounting system and the other operational data files. The following morning she was there again, and this time she included a study of Fred Store's activities in the warehouse. She even remembered to ask him about his gardening duties and complimented him on how attractive the property looked. This pleased Fred immensely, and caused him to lose his reservations about the impending computer system, and to "spill the beans" about how the current system worked at his end, including all the quirks.

Tom had told Fred that there was no possibility of the computer replacing him, but Fred had some doubts about how he would fit in. Sarah also assured Fred that his job was secure and pointed out that the new system would do much the same things as the current manual system, only more efficiently. The net result, as far as Fred was concerned, would probably mean time for an extra half hour each day at landscaping, which also pleased Fred.

In Tom Sayles' office, Sarah was able to observe Tom in action on the phone first hand. She could see how essential Joan Wright's current data files were to Tom's buy/sell decisions. Sarah also saw how inconvenient it was for Tom to continually have to talk to Joan about inventory when dealing with customers and suppliers. The image of Tom at his large desk, with open IC catalogues and at least two phones going, was hard to forget. No doubt about it, thought Sarah, just one phone and a computer terminal would be a big improvement.

That evening, at home, Sarah thought about SMS's system. Once more the problem was the accounting system. It's amazing, she thought; I'm supposed to be an expert in computer data base systems, but I keep running into accounting systems I don't fully understand. Her problem was the way the accounts were updated following purchase and sales of parts. But it was the fact that four different accounts had to be updated following a sale that really puzzled her (we saw this in Figure 3.4). Next day she decided that she had better spend some time in the library at Cybertek, looking at some accounting texts. She already knew from experience that looking for the answer in a data base text was a waste of time.

As we saw in Chapter 2, Sarah had long ago taken a course in accounting, but had forgotten most of it. However, it was slowly coming back. As she gained experience, it became increasingly evident to her that data bases in business contained a great deal of accounting data.

After a solid day of looking into the accounting techniques for purchase and sale of goods at hypothetical textbook wholesale firms, Sarah finally saw the light. When goods are purchased (for resale), the value of the inventory must climb. But either the firm's cash must decrease by the same amount if the goods are purchased for cash, or the firm's accounts receivable must increase by the same amount if the goods are bought on credit. Either way, there is no effect on the firm's equity, and this is the key to the matter. Since the firm's equity breaks down into revenue less expenditures, no expenditure account can be affected.

This is what had puzzled Sarah. Apparently, parts are initially purchased, but there is no associated entry in the expenditures account. The purchase of the parts is not an expenditure to obtain revenue until the parts are actually sold. When the parts are bought, the cash asset to buy them is simply converted to the parts asset in inventory. If bought on credit, a debt liability increases (accounts payable) to cover the increase in the inventory asset.

The reason for the four account entries to post a sale of parts in the ledger now became clear to Sarah, and she drew a diagram showing all the accounts that made up the ledger. Accounts contributing a balance to the asset side she placed on the left, and those from the equity/liability side, including revenue and expenditure accounts, she placed on the right, as shown in Figure 3.3. Sarah now understood that if parts are sold, the resulting drop in inventory asset value must cause equity to fall, in the form of an increase in expenditures. But there will be revenue from the sale, which will increase assets, either as cash from the sale, or as an increase in accounts receivable. This increase in assets is matched by an increase in equity, in the form of the increase in revenue. Thus equity increases because of revenue and decreases because of expenditure. The net increase of equity would then be revenue minus expenditure, or sale price for the parts minus cost of the parts.

This was the heart of the accounting system. Unless you understood it there was no way you could design a data base and associated processing for a firm like SMS.

Data Base Considerations

With the overall picture clear in her head, Sarah's next task was to design the data base or data bases. She had to show how the firm's data would be used in much the same way as with the manual system, augmented by uses that currently were prohibitive in terms of time.

The major design question was one data base or two, for she still remembered the warning in all the textbooks about trying to set up one master data base for all of a firm's operational data. However, experience was beginning to teach Sarah just why that warning was there. Clearly, if the firm was large and complex, the amount of processing required of the operational data would also be very large. Thus, if you did succeed in designing a master data base for the entire firm, the programming effort required to implement all the programs would be very large, and would take a great deal of time. But by the time the system was ready, it was very likely that things would have changed at the firm (in a complex organization, management usually reorganizes things about every six months). As a result, the new system would no longer fit and would probably fail. Thus the standard approach of implementing a data base and associated application software only for a specific and manageable area of the firm's operations is more likely to succeed.

There was an obvious drawback to the one-data-base-at-a-time approach, however. especially when dealing with a small firm. Suppose that Sarah decided to do things in two steps, with two distinct data bases. The first step would be a data base for everything directly connected with purchases, inventory, part types, and sales, with associated manipulation software, but with all other matters left for manual operation. This would be very trying for the people at SMS. For example, some of the general ledger accounts would be in the data base, such as inventory, accounts receivable and accounts payable (since these were directly connected with sales and purchases), whereas others, such as cash, would not. Thus part of the posting to the general ledger for any journal transaction would be done by computer and part would be done manually.

As far as Sarah could see, designing a clean separation between the computer data and the manual data would be very difficult in a first step. And later, when the remaining manual data was implemented as a second data base, some, and perhaps many, of the original programs for the first data base would have to be thrown out and replaced by programs that managed both data bases.

Sarah could see that the final result of this two stage approach, if all went well, would be very appealing in theory. Some programs would manipulate data base A, and some would manipulate data base B, and some would manipulate both data base A and B. She had seen diagrams of situations like this in text books. All very well, she thought, but getting from a situation where you have data base A with associated programs, to a situation where you have data bases A and B and associated programs, is going to be an involved affair. It was obvious to her that Tom Sayles had a turnkey system in mind, with everything manual one day, and everything computerized the next day. Certainly there should be no lengthy period, as at most large firms, during which a steady on-going conversion from manual to computer systems takes place. Sarah decided to discuss the problem with her boss, Peter Stone.

Data Base Design Options at SMS

In his office at Cybernetics, Peter Stone listened to Sarah's analysis of the problem. Sarah had learned not to bring problems to her boss. She was being paid to generate solutions, after all. When she had finished her analysis, Sarah came out with three strategies for handling SMS's conversion to data base management:

(a) The way things are done at larger firms. One data base to begin with for purchasing and selling and associated software. Later, a second data base for remaining general ledger accounts and software for both data bases.

(b) The way she had done it at Lucky Strike Industries. One data base for the entire firm and associated software. A turnkey system that once installed, would require only minimum maintenance.

(c) A hybrid approach, suitable for a small firm like SMS. Two data bases would be designed initially, but no software would be implemented until both data base designs were complete. The separation into two data bases would be merely a matter of convenience. One data base would deal with purchases, sales, inventory, part types, and closely related entities. The other data base would deal with remaining general ledger accounts and the journal, and it would be similar to that designed for Lucky Strike Industries. Software would be classified into the following:

(1) Programs for the sales/purchase/inventory data base alone.

(2) Programs for the general ledger/journal data base alone.

(3) Programs for both data bases.

Although Peter Stone thought that some additional strategies were also possible, Sarah's three strategies more or less covered the options. He agreed with Sarah that the first option was out, if for no other reason than that the customer would like neither the inconvenience it would cause nor the extra expense.

Peter found that choosing between option b and c was much harder. He had some misgivings about the use of two data bases in option c, as he felt that the separation between the two data bases would not be all that clean. After all, there would be conceptual files in both data bases that were essentially accounts in the general ledger. Nevertheless, if any subdivision into two data bases was useful, it was the one that Sarah had proposed. He conceded that since the business of SMS was the purchase and sale of components, a separate data base for this would be useful, especially since most daily information retrieval would be directed at this data base. Finally, experience had taught him that it always pays to break down the work into steps. As a result, he favored option c, which was also the option that Sarah preferred.

Sarah's next task would be the design of the two data bases. With her experience at Lucky Strike behind her, she felt that the second data base for the general ledger and the journal would be a relatively easy affair. The meat of the design problem would be in the first data base for purchase and sale of parts. It took her almost a week to design that data base. In the next section, we will look at the steps that Sarah followed in its design.

Design of the Data Base for Parts, Sales and Purchases

To decide what data belonged in each data base, Sarah first drew up a crude data dictionary showing most of the fields that would be needed. She was able to do this from her notes taken at SMS. Then she made up a data/process matrix, with the fields along one side of the matrix and the processes along the adjacent side, so that she could see which processes affected which fields. She was able to confirm that the sales, inventory, purchase, and part type data formed a reasonably natural grouping. She had been able to discern this without the data/process matrix, because of her bird's eye view of the firm.

Sarah wondered if such a convenient bird's eye view would be available with a very large firm. Having to rely on a data/process matrix alone as a guide to grouping fields into data bases, a technique described in many textbooks, gave her an uneasy feeling. It would probably work, she thought, but wondered how many times you would have to rearrange that data in the matrix before the data groupings become obvious. Seen from her perspective, the data/process matrix seemed like a poor crutch to help those who could not understand the firm.

Sarah began her design with three obvious entities: the suppliers, the customers, and the part types. Each of these would have a conceptual file. The supplier file would have a supplier number as primary key, and remaining fields would contain items like address, telephone number, and name of contact person. Similar fields would be needed with the customer file, plus a credit limit field. With the part type file there would be an identifying part type number as primary key, and fields would describe the type part. Sarah decided to leave the details of all these fields until later and to begin with a basic entity-relationship diagram for these conceptual files. She drew the three boxes at the top in Figure 3.5.

Then she considered the most obvious relationships involving these entities. For any given supplier, at any instant, there would be parts on order. In addition, for any given customer, there would be parts that the customer was expected to

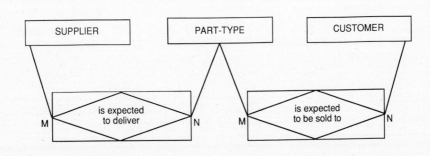

FIGURE 3.5. Data base for covering suppliers (of ICs), the part types involved, the customers, what part types are on order (expected to be delivered), and what part types telephone agreement has been reached to sell (is expected to be sold to) to customers. This is an initial Entity-Relationship diagram. A Bachman structure diagram is shown in Figure 3.6.

order—that is committed parts, as a result of telephone conversations between the customers and Tom Sayles. In the manual system Joan kept track of both parts on order from suppliers and parts that SMS was committed to sell. These considerations allowed Sarah to complete the E-R diagram as shown in Figure 3.5.

Sarah then refined the E-R diagram into a Bachman diagram, as shown in Figure 3.6. This gave her two new conceptual files. These were the PARTS-ON-ORDER file, a record of which listed the quantity of a part type on order from a supplier, and the COMMITTED-PART-SALES file, a record of which listed the quantity of a part type that a customer had verbally agreed to order.

The data base in Figure 3.6 did not involve any accounting data. Whenever a purchase order went out to a supplier, the PART-ON-ORDER file would be updated to reflect new parts on order. When the parts actually arrived, this information would be deleted from the PARTS-ON- ORDER file, and inventory and other files would be updated. Similarly, when a customer agreed to order parts from SMS, an entry would be made in the COMMITTED-PART-SALES file, and the entry would be removed when the parts were actually sold.

This data base, as designed so far, would be useful to Tom when dealing with customers and suppliers on the telephone. If a customer called asking for part type P77, Tom could look in

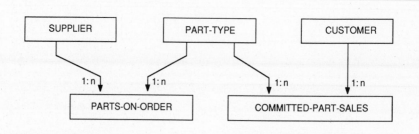

FIGURE 3.6 Bachman structure diagram showing conceptual files for data base in Figure 3.5. There are two many-to-many relationships. Each record of the PARTS-ON-ORDER file gives the quantity of a type of part on order. Each record of the COMMITTED-PART-SALES file gives the quantity of a part type that SMS has agreed to sell, without yet receiving a purchase order.

the inventory file (or files) to see what was in stock, but he could also look in COMMITTED-PARTS-SALES, to see what P77 parts were already committed for sale. If not enough P77 parts were in stock, given prior sale commitments, Tom could then look in PARTS-ON-ORDER, to see if it was worth the risk of accepting the customer's order. Actually all this information can be integrated into a view, as we shall see shortly.

Next Sarah turned her attention to the inventory file, aware that it would be involved in the general ledger accounts. Essentially she needed something like that shown in Figure 3.7. Whenever parts were acquired from a supplier via a given purchase order, there had to be an entry for each part type on that purchase order. We see (Figure 3.7) that purchase order 17 involved the order of 2000 P16 parts, and 1000 P56 parts. The amount for each type of part ordered (and delivered) is shown in dollars, as a debit to the general ledger. Thus the file is a general ledger account.

Notice that the file also contains information about what happens to inventory as parts are sold out of inventory. During the ensuing months, some of the P56 parts from purchase order

PUR-ORDER#	SALES-ORDER#	PART-TYPE#	QTY	AMOUNT	D/C
PUR17	—	P16	2,000	$6,000	DEBIT
PUR17	—	P56	1,000	$3,000	DEBIT
PUR17	SALE42	P56	200	$600	CREDIT
PUR21	—	P85	2,000	$8,000	DEBIT
PUR17	SALE55	P56	400	$1,200	CREDIT
PUR21	SALE62	P85	1,000	$4,000	CREDIT
PUR24	—	P56	1,500	$6,000	DEBIT
PUR17	SALE64	P56	300	$900	CREDIT

FIGURE 3.7. The essence of the inventory file, which, as shown above, unfortunately does not have a structure suitable for a conceptual data base file. The above file is also a general ledger account and tracks all increases and decreases in inventory, down to the detail of sales of a part type purchased with an individual purchase order. For example, we can see that on purchase order 17, there were acquired 1,000 P56 ICs at $3 each. Then (on sales order 42) 200 of these parts, costing $600, were sold; later (sales order 55) another 400 of the P56 parts from purchase order 17 were sold. Later (purchase order 24) more P56 parts are acquired. Later still, P56 parts were sold under sales order 64, but they did not come from the batch acquired under purchase order 24.

17 will be sold in smaller batches. For example, sales order 42 includes 200 of the P56 parts originally ordered under purchase order 17. These has to be an entry, including a dollar amount involved for each removal of parts from the warehouse—that is, from inventory. And notice the dollar amount involved is in terms of cost of the parts, and not sale price.

In consequence, if we want to know how many P56 parts are in the warehouse, as a result of a given purchase order number, such as PUR17, we sum what went in, and subtract what went out. Similarly, we can get the dollar amount by subtracting what went out from what sent in for a given purchase order number. What goes out is shown as a credit.

The file in Figure 3.7 covers the essentials of what goes on in inventory and in the accounting of inventory changes. Unfortunately, the file is a poor candidate for a conceptual data base file.

In the file in Figure 3.7, we are dealing with two different entities (or events) in one file—namely, increases in inventory and decreases in inventory. With an increase we must enter the purchase order used to get the parts from the supplier. With a decrease we must again give this purchase order number, plus the sales order number of the sales order used by the customer to buy the parts. This should be clear from Figure 3.7. With some reluctance, Sarah decided that the only thing to do was separate the increases from the decreases, so that there would be two distinct conceptual files. These files are shown in Figure 3.8a.

The two new conceptual files to handle inventory are INVENTORY-DEBIT for increases in inventory, and INVENTORY-CREDIT for decreases in inventory. The account of a particular increase in inventory will be identified by the purchase order number (P-O#) and the part type involved (PART-TYPE#), so that these two fields also serve as a composite primary key. It should be clear that there will be a 1:n relationship between INVENTORY-DEBIT and INVENTORY-CREDIT, since, for a given increase in inventory, there will usually be a number of decreases until all of that increased inventory is sold off.

Notice that there is a unit-cost field in INVENTORY-DEBIT. To get the value of any increase in inventory, you have to

P-O#	PART-TYPE#	QTY.	UNIT-COST
PUR17	P56	1,000	$3.00
PUR21	P85	2,000	$4.00
PUR24	P56	1,500	$4.00
PUR28	P85	3,000	$3.00

INVENTORY-DEBIT

P-O#	PART-TYPE#	S-O#	QTY.
PUR 17	P56	SALE42	200
PUR17	P56	SALE55	400
PUR21	P85	SALE61	800
PUR17	P56	SALE72	300
PUR21	P85	SALE67	900
PUR28	P85	SALE72	800
PUR17	P56	SALE74	100
PUR28	P85	SALE42	2,000
PUR24	P56	SALE72	900

INVENTORY-CREDIT

(a) The essential inventory file from Figure 3.7 is broken down into two inventory account files, each of which will be a general ledger account. INVENTORY-DEBIT accounts for all increases in inventory as a result of purchase orders to suppliers. INVENTORY-CREDIT accounts for all decreases in the inventory as a result of sales orders from customers. Each record in INVENTORY-CREDIT depletes, in whole or in part, the inventory increase due to a record in INVENTORY-DEBIT. There is thus in 1:n relationship between these two inventory files. When doing a trial balance, the figure QTY * UNIT-COST is used for each entry in both files; for INVENTORY-CREDIT the UNIT-COST figure is obtained from the parent INVENTORY-DEBIT record. Items such as dates, customer name, supplier name, and so on, are expected to be available from cross-references.

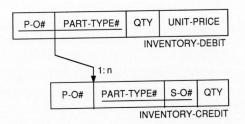

(b) Extended Bachman diagram for the core inventory files, which are also general ledger inventory accounts, from (a). As the design proceeds, changes may be made to the record compositions.

FIGURE 3.8. Core Inventory files (continued)

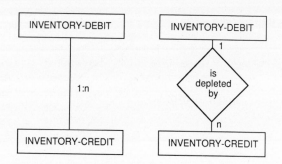

(c) Bachman and Entity-Relationship diagrams for the core inventory files from (a). We can use these for further design when we are still unsure about some of the individual fields.

FIGURE 3.8.   Core Inventory files

multiply the quantity of parts by the unit cost. The system will do this when it is using the INVENTORY-DEBIT file as part of a trial balance. These is no unit cost field in INVENTORY-CREDIT. If 200 of part P56 are sold, and entered into INVENTORY-CREDIT, to get the amount involved in dollars for the cost of those parts originally, the unit cost field from the parent INVENTORY-DEBIT file is used ($3,00 in this case). This unit cost figure is then multiplied by the quantity sold to get the cost of the goods sold. Naturally, during a trial balance, the system must make use of the quantity sold in an INVENTORY-CREDIT record, multiplied by the UNIT-COST value in the parent INVENTORY-DEBIT record as well, to get the cost of the goods sold, and thus the dollar amount by which inventory has decreased.

Readers who are familiar with functional dependencies should be able to see that it would be wrong to include a UNIT-COST field in INVENTORY-CREDIT, since such a field would be functionally dependent on the composite field P-O# PART-TYPE#, which is not the primary key. Consequently, it could lead to inconsistency if UNIT-COST in the two files for the same P-O# and PART-TYPE# should differ.

It would even be wrong to include an AMOUNT field in INVENTORY-CREDIT. This is a rare example of an implicit functional dependency. Dividing AMOUNT by QTY gives the unit cost, which is not functionally dependent on the primary key fields of INVENTORY-CREDIT but on the composite P-O# PART-TYPE#. In addition, AMOUNT would be functionally dependent on P-O# PART-TYPE# QTY, which is not the primary key. The design in Figure 3.8a avoids all such problems, although Sarah is still not sure that all essential fields are included. She decides to continue with the design, and for the sake of having more compact designs for these two vital inventory files, makes up an extended Bachman diagram (Figure 3.8b), as well as plain Bachman and entity- relationship diagrams, as shown in Figure 3.8c.

At this point Sarah decides to check on how well the two inventory files will mesh with the files PARTS-ON ORDER and COMMITTED-PART-SALES in Figure 3.6. One frequent use for these files will be getting information to Tom about what parts are in inventory coupled to what is on order and what is verbally committed for sale. Essentially what Tom needs is a view of the data base, or an external data base, like CONSOLI-DATED-INVENTORY (Figure 3.9). From this file, for a given part type, from a given supplier, Tom can see what is in inventory, what is on order, and what is committed.

Sarah feels that most of the data for the view CONSOLI-DATED-INVENTORY can be derived from PARTS-ON-ORDER, COMMITTED-PARTS-SALES, and the two inventory files. However, some parts of the puzzle are still missing. As far as she can see, from the inventory files alone, it is not possible to determine the supplier of the parts in inventory, which a customer, as well as Tom, would want to know. When I get them designed, the supplier number value will likely come from files related to the inventory files, Sarah thinks. She will decide the questions of how to have CONSOLIDATED-INVENTORY generated from underlying conceptual files later. It may be by means of a single well-thought out SQL expression or by means of a separate program.

This leads Sarah to the files that relate to the inventory files. Inventory is clearly affected by what goes into inventory (recorded in INVENTORY-DEBIT) and what comes out of inventory (recorded in INVENTORY-CREDIT). But what goes into inventory must be purchased on credit, and what goes out of inventory is sold, also on credit. Whenever goods are bought

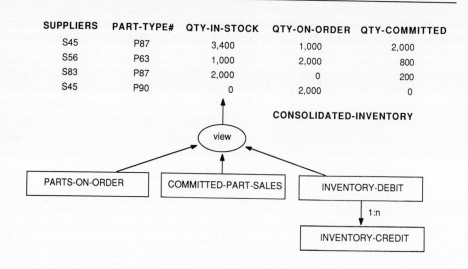

SUPPLIERS	PART-TYPE#	QTY-IN-STOCK	QTY-ON-ORDER	QTY-COMMITTED
S45	P87	3,400	1,000	2,000
S56	P63	1,000	2,000	800
S83	P87	2,000	0	200
S45	P90	0	2,000	0

FIGURE 3.9. The consolidated inventory file (top) is not stored as part of the data base, but is computed from data in the core inventory files (INVENTORY-CREDIT and INVENTORY-DEBIT) and from the files describing parts on order from suppliers and parts committed for sale (See Figures 3.6 and 3.8). It can thus be interpreted as a view of the data base, although it remains to be seen whether it can be specified in terms of an SQL expression or whether it needs a specific program to generate it. The file will be used by Tom Sayles in discussing possible purchase and sales orders on the telephone. Note that he needs the quantity in stock from each specific supplier. He will not fill a sales order for $1,000 P87 parts, for example, by sending the customer 600 made by S45 and 400 made by S83, at least not without the customer's agreement. Thus a consolidated inventory file is necessary for daily business decisions.

on credit, accounts payables are affected, and whenever goods are sold on credit, accounts receivable are affected. Accordingly, accounts payable and accounts receivable must be closely related to the inventory files. Sarah first looks at accounts payable.

Sarah reasons along these lines. Suppose that Tom places an order with a supplier using a purchase order numbered PUR17. This purchase order could be for three different types of parts, so that it will have three lines. In this case it could be for $3000 of part type P56, $3,000 of part type P87, and $2,000 of part type P17, for a total order worth $8,000. When the goods are delivered, accounts payable will increase by $8,000, so that there must be a record entered into the accounts payable file for this amount, giving the purchase order involved, the supplier's invoice number, date, and so on.

There has to be a corresponding update of $8,000 worth of inventory in the inventory files. However, there will not be a single update. There will be three updates, since it is individual part types and their costs that matter in inventory. Three different part types were purchased, and so there will be three updates to INVENTORY-DEBIT. Remember that INVENTORY-DEBIT records increases in inventory, a record showing the increase in any type of part. This means that there must be a 1:n relationship between ACCOUNTS-PAYABLE and INVENTORY-DEBIT, as illustrated in Figure 3.10. An ACCOUNTS-PAYABLE record records the total increase in debt as a result of purchasing the parts. There is a single record

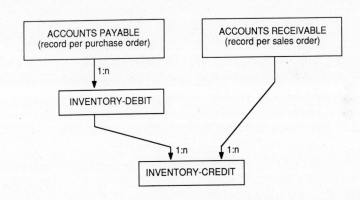

FIGURE 3.10. Showing how the accounts payable and accounts receivable files will interface with the core inventory files. ACCOUNTS-PAYABLE and ACCOUNTS-RECEIVABLE will be general ledger files used in trial balances and balance sheet generation. Thus all four files above are part of the general ledger. An ACCOUNTS-PAYABLE record will give the total dollar value for a purchase order (and thus purchase invoice). Since an order will usually be for more than one type of component, there will be many INVENTORY-DEBIT records for an ACCOUNTS-PAYABLE record. An ACCOUNTS-RECEIVABLE record will give the total dollar value of a sales order (and thus sales invoice). Since an order will be for more than one type of part, there will usually be many INVENTORY- CREDIT records for one ACCOUNT-RECEIVABLE record.

in INVENTORY-DEBIT for each line of the purchase order, causing the increase in accounts payable.

Now suppose that some parts are sold via a given sales order, for example sales order 42, for 200 of part type P56 for $1,000, and 1,000 of part type P85 for $8,000, for a total of $9,000. Clearly, accounts receivable must be updated with an entry to reflect $9,000 for sales order 42. However, there will be two entries to INVENTORY-CREDIT, showing a reduction of P56 parts and P85 parts—that is, an new record in INVENTORY-CREDIT for each line of sales order 42. Accordingly, there will be a 1:n relationship between the conceptual file ACCOUNTS-RECEIVABLE and INVENTORY-CREDIT, as shown in Figure 3.10.

This does not appear too complex. However, there are further complexities. For every entry of an increase in accounts payable, SMS will sooner or later send a remittance to the supplier to clear the debt, or several remittances, thus paying off the debt in installments. A record will have to be kept of such remittances, so that at any given instant the amount owed due to accounts payable will be the sum of the totals originally recorded in ACCOUNTS-PAYABLE less the sum of the remittances. Sarah decides to have an additional conceptual file for remittances sent to pay off payables debt, called PAYABLES-REMITTANCES. Clearly, at any given instant, for a given record in ACCOUNTS-PAYABLE, there can be zero or more records in PAYABLES-REMITTANCES, each recording a reduction in the amount recorded as owing in the ACCOUNTS-PAYABLE record. There will thus be a 1:n relationship between ACCOUNTS-PAYABLE and RECEIVABLE-REMITTANCES, as illustrated in Figure 3.11.

As well as remittances sent by SMS to its suppliers, each customer who has had an order for parts executed by SMS, and who has a corresponding entry in the ACCOUNTS-RECEIVABLE file, will send one or more remittances to pay off its debt due to that order. Each of these remittances will be recorded in a RECEIVABLES-REMITTANCES file as a distinct record. Thus, as with payables, there will a 1:n relationship between ACCOUNTS-RECEIVABLE and RECEIVABLES-REMITTANCES, as shown in Figure 3.11.

We can look at the six conceptual files in Figure 3.11 as forming three close groups. One group consists of the two

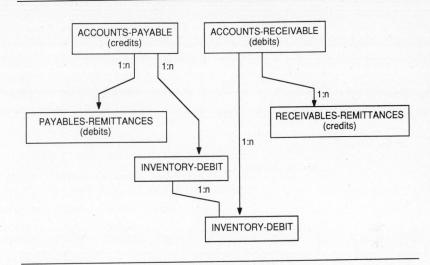

FIGURE 3.11. The data base described in Figure 3.10 does not fully describe the data connected with accounts payable and accounts receivable. It does not take remittances on payables and receivables into account. The ACCOUNTS-PAYABLE file will list entries for amounts owed because of receipt of invoices or fulfillment of a purchase order. The amount owing may be paid off in portions, each portion being described by an entry or record in PAYABLES-REMITTANCES. Thus, for any ACCOUNTS-PAYABLE record, there may be many payments remitted to the supplier to pay it off, and hence many related records in the file PAYABLES-REMITTANCES. Similarly, the records in RECEIVABLES- REMITTANCES describe the payments made by a customer to eliminate debts listed in ACCOUNTS-RECEIVABLE. Again, there will be a one-to-many relationship between ACCOUNTS-RECEIVABLE and RECEIVABLES-REMITTANCES. All the files shown above describe general ledger accounts.

inventory files, which we have already examined in some detail (Figure 3.8), another group consists of the two payables files, and the last group consists of the two receivables files. These groups correspond to the general ledger inventory accounts, the general ledger payables accounts, and the general ledger receivables accounts. There is important detail here, and so we first look more closely at how the ACCOUNTS-PAYABLE file relates to the INVENTORY-DEBIT and PAYABLES-REMIT-TANCES files (Figure 3.12); later we look at how the ACCOUNTS-RECEIVABLE file relates to the INVENTORY-CREDIT and RECEIVABLES-REMITTANCES files.

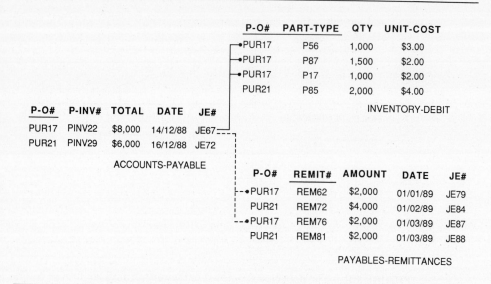

P-O#	PART-TYPE	QTY	UNIT-COST
PUR17	P56	1,000	$3.00
PUR17	P87	1,500	$2.00
PUR17	P17	1,000	$2.00
PUR21	P85	2,000	$4.00

INVENTORY-DEBIT

P-O#	P-INV#	TOTAL	DATE	JE#
PUR17	PINV22	$8,000	14/12/88	JE67
PUR21	PINV29	$6,000	16/12/88	JE72

ACCOUNTS-PAYABLE

P-O#	REMIT#	AMOUNT	DATE	JE#
PUR17	REM62	$2,000	01/01/89	JE79
PUR21	REM72	$4,000	01/02/89	JE84
PUR17	REM76	$2,000	01/03/89	JE87
PUR21	REM81	$2,000	01/03/89	JE88

PAYABLES-REMITTANCES

FIGURE 3.12. Showing details of records in ACCOUNTS-PAYABLE, IN-VENTORY-DEBIT and PAYABLES-REMITTANCES. Suppose that SMS purchases parts P56, P87 and P17 on purchase order 17 (invoice 22). The total cost may be entered in ACCOUNTS-PAYABLE as $8,000. For each part in the order, there is an entry in INVENTORY-DEBIT, and for each remittance for the order, there is an entry in PAYABLES-REMITTANCES.

Referring to Figure 3.12, we can trace the accounts receivable entry for $8,000 due to purchase order 17 (PUR17) and purchase invoice 22 (PINV22). When the goods were received, an entry was made in the journal for the $8,000, and this was journal entry 67 (JE67); in addition, a record was inserted in ACCOUNTS-PAYABLE for this transaction, showing $8,000 on PUR17. The purchase order number (P-O#) field identifies the transaction and so can serve as primary key in ACCOUNTS-PAYABLE.

Purchase order 17 was made of up line orders for part types P56, P87, and P17. For each of these, there is an entry in INVENTORY-DEBIT, showing the cost of each individual line order for part types. Rather than give total cost of a line order and the quantity of parts, we give the quantity of parts and unit cost. Thus we see that out of the total $8,000 for purchase order PUR17, 1000*3 or $3,000 was paid for the P56 parts.

At this point Sarah notices an interfile dependency, and remembers that it is a common type often mentioned in text books. The record for PUR17 in ACCOUNTS-PAYABLE has three related records in INVENTORY-CREDIT, namely the records, with PUR17, for part types P56, P87, and P17. The ACCOUNTS-PAYABLES record shows the sum of the costs of the quantities involved for these three part types, namely:

$$8,000 = 1,000 * 3.00 + 1,500 * 2.00 + 1,000 * 2.00$$

Thus the values in QTY and UNIT-COST in INVENTORY-DEBIT determine the value ($8,000) in TOTAL in ACCOUNTS-PAYABLE. Strictly, TOTAL should be removed, since the value in TOTAL in a parent record can always be computed from the sum of the QTY*UNIT-COST products for its child records. However, notwithstanding the arguments in the text books for eliminating such dependencies, Sarah decides that the arguments for retaining the TOTAL field in this particular case are stronger. The deciding arguments are the following:

(a) The fields in these records, once inserted, are unlikely ever to be updated, so that the only inconsistency that could occur would be at the time of insertion, and the insertion program could be programmed to check for any such inconsistency (and refuse the entry if it found one).

(b) Accounting systems in general are full of interfile dependencies, since accountants like to have multiple entries of the same thing as a means of checking and verification. Thus if there should slip in an inconsistency because of this dependency, the general ledger account would fail the trial balance, which would permit the inconsistency to be detected.

This leads Sarah to digress somewhat in her thoughts. There seem to be two totally different philosophies at work in the accounting and data base fields, she thought. In the accounting field, the basic idea seems to be permit the possibility of inconsistency, but design things so that such an inconsistency can be easily detected, for example, with trial balances, and then can be rectified. The advantage of this approach is that both errors of inconsistency and inaccuracy can be detected. In the data base approach, on the other hand, the idea is to prevent inconsistency from occurring in the first place, by having no dependencies. The disadvantage to this, from the accounting point of view, is that although you may be preventing the data from being inconsistent, you do not necessarily prevent inaccuracy, and you make it more difficult to detect such inaccuracies should they occur.

For example, suppose that the data base in Figure 3.12 (or Figure 3.11) stood alone, and did not have the TOTAL field in ACCOUNTS- PAYABLE. The TOTAL value would be determined from the sum of the QTY*UNIT-COST products in the child INVENTORY-DEBIT records instead, and would be acceptable according to orthodox data base theory. But now, suppose that there was an error in entering the UNIT-COST value for one of those child records. There would still be no inconsistency. Nevertheless, any TOTAL value deduced would also be in error, and what is worse, there would be no way of detecting the inaccuracy from the data in the data base. Thus, with dependency theory, the price of a consistent data base is possible undetectable inaccuracy.

Accounting is an old established profession, muses Sarah, going back centuries. Long and hard experience has probably taught them to do things the way they do. And right there she hits on a simple principle, not found in data base texts.

"When dealing with accounting data in data base design, other things being equal if there is a conflict between what accounting practice would dictate and what data base dependency theory would dictate, always give accounting practice the benefit of the doubt."

Sarah decides to leave the TOTAL field in ACCOUNTS-PAYABLE where it is.

Continuing with the ramifications of the accounts payable entry for the $8,000 on purchase order PUR17 (Figure 3.12), in the course of time, SMS makes remittances to the supplier—first $2,000 (remittance 62), and later another $2,000 (remittance 76). To find out what SMS actually owes on purchase order 17, the record for PUR17 must first be retrieved from ACCOUNTS-PAYABLE in order to extract the TOTAL value of $8,000 for the original order. Then the child PAYABLES-REMITTANCES records have to be retrieved, and the AMOUNT values summed, giving, in this case, a value of $4,000 for the total remitted to the supplier. The amount remaining to be paid therefore, is $8,000 − $4,000, or $4,000. This $4,000 figure is the amount still owing on purchase order 17.

Once more SARAH notices that you cannot find out from this data base who is the supplier of the parts ordered in purchase order PUR17. Obviously, this data base will eventually have to be linked to the data base in Figure 3.6, which contains the conceptual file SUPPLIER. However, that can wait. Next, we have to look more closely at how ACCOUNTS-RECEIVABLE interacts with INVENTORY-CREDIT and RECEIVABLES-REMITTANCES.

This interaction is illustrated in Figure 3.13. Suppose that SMS receives a sales order, sales order 42 (or SALE42) for delivery of 200 P56 at a unit price of $5.00 and 2,000 P85 parts at

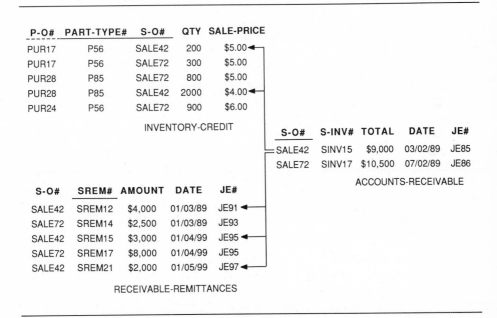

P-O#	PART-TYPE#	S-O#	QTY	SALE-PRICE
PUR17	P56	SALE42	200	$5.00
PUR17	P56	SALE72	300	$5.00
PUR28	P85	SALE72	800	$5.00
PUR28	P85	SALE42	2000	$4.00
PUR24	P56	SALE72	900	$6.00

INVENTORY-CREDIT

S-O#	S-INV#	TOTAL	DATE	JE#
SALE42	SINV15	$9,000	03/02/89	JE85
SALE72	SINV17	$10,500	07/02/89	JE86

ACCOUNTS-RECEIVABLE

S-O#	SREM#	AMOUNT	DATE	JE#
SALE42	SREM12	$4,000	01/03/89	JE91
SALE72	SREM14	$2,500	01/03/89	JE93
SALE42	SREM15	$3,000	01/04/99	JE95
SALE72	SREM17	$8,000	01/04/99	JE95
SALE42	SREM21	$2,000	01/05/99	JE97

RECEIVABLE-REMITTANCES

FIGURE 3.13. Showing details of records in ACCOUNTS-RECEIVABLE, INVENTORY-DEBIT and RECEIVABLES-REMITTANCES. Suppose that SALE42 involves sale of parts P56 (originally acquired on PUR17) and P85 (acquired on PUR28). The sale and total revenue from the sale is entered in ACCOUNTS-RECEIVABLE. There is also an entry for each type of component involved—in INVENTORY-DEBIT showing sale price per unit IC. If later, three remittances (of $4,000, $3,000 and $2,000) are sent by the customer to pay off the debt incurred, each is entered in RECEIVABLES-REMITTANCES.

a unit price of $4.00. This means that the order is worth 200*5 + 2,000*4 or $9,000. An entry for this amount will go into accounts receivable, since the customer buys on credit, following the original entry for the transaction in the journal (journal entry JE85). This journal entry number will also be contained in the accounts receivable records, as shown in Figure 3.13. In addition, there will be an entry, or a record, in INVENTORY-CREDIT for each of the types of part, that is, for each line-item in the sales order (or customer purchase order). In this example, we need an INVENTORY-CREDIT record for the 200 P56 parts and another record for the 2,000 P85 parts. These records indicate the extent by which parts inventory has been reduced due to sales of parts. Notice that INVENTORY-CREDIT now has an additional field compared with the first version in Figure 3.8. This is the SALE-PRICE field, which clearly belongs in INVENTORY-CREDIT.

SALE-PRICE is not functionally dependent on PART-TYPE#, since the sales price of P85 parts, for example, can vary, as is the case in Figure 3.13. SALES-PRICE is functionally dependent on the primary key field, which is a composite of PART-TYPE# and S-O# (sales order number). Or is it? If it is, each record describes sale of a particular part type via a particular sales order number. But what about the following possibility? On sales order 72 there is a line item for P85 parts, originally bought on purchase order 28 (PUR28), as shown in Figure 3.13. Suppose now that there was also a line item for further P85 parts on sales order 72, but originating with purchase order PUR33 (not shown in Figure 3.13). In other words Tom is selling two different batches of P85 parts, possibly from two different suppliers, to the same customer. If that could happen, then the primary key field would have to be P-O# PART-TYPE# S-O#.

Sarah immediately phones SMS, and asks Joan Wright if such a thing can happen. Joan says it can, but only if the two batches of parts come from the same supplier originally. "Tom will not mix suppliers on an order for a given type of part," explains Joan.

This intelligence definitely means that the primary key for INVENTORY-CREDIT is not, after all, what was deduced for Figure 3.8, but a composite of P-O#, PART-TYPE#, and S-O#. But what about the restriction that where PART-TYPE# and S-O# are the same, then the original supplier must be the same?

That looks like it could be an important functional dependency, but since Sarah is fairly sure that supplier number (SUP#) does not belong in INVENTORY-CREDIT, she decides that the restriction involved will have to be handled by means of an integrity constraint.

Readers should recall that it is the cost of the parts that is used in computing inventory values, and not sale prices. Accordingly, when the program responsible for computing inventory values is determining the value in inventory of P56 parts purchased originally under purchase order 17 (PUR17), it first obtains the value of the parts originally entered into inventory, as the product of UNIT-COST and QTY from the record for PUR17 in INVENTORY-DEBIT (Figure 3.12). It then subtracts from this the value of all P56 (reduction) records in INVENTORY-CREDIT, that is, the child records of the PUR17 parent INVENTORY-DEBIT record (Figure 33.8a), using QTY values from the child records, and the UNIT-COST field from the parent record—not the SALE- PRICE values from the child records.

Continuing with the design in Figure 3.13, for any given sales order, whose value is entered in an ACCOUNTS-RECEIV-ABLE record, there will be remittances sent from the customer from time to time, thus gradually eliminating the debt to SMS. For each remittance there will be a journal entry, and a record in RECEIVABLES-REMITTANCES that gives the amount, the sales order to which it applies, the amount involved and the date, as well as the journal entry number for the transaction.

To obtain the amount owing to SMS for any invoice that is not fully paid up, the TOTAL value from the ACCOUNTS-RECEIVABLE record for that invoice is first extracted. Then from this TOTAL value the sum of the AMOUNT values in each child RECEIVABLES-REMITTANCES record is subtracted. The 1:n relationship between ACCOUNTS-RECEIV-ABLE and RECEIVABLES-REMITTANCES is supported by the sales order number (S-O#) field involved, and not the invoice number. (However, an alternative design could use the invoice number, but the change is not a trivial one and affects the entire final data base.)

Sarah also notices the same interfile dependency involving the TOTAL field in ACCOUNTS-RECEIVABLE-RECEIV-ABLE as appeared in ACCOUNTS- PAYABLE in Figure 3.12. The TOTAL value can be computed from the sum of the

QTY∗SALE-PRICE values in the child INVENTORY-CREDIT records. Thus there is a redundancy caused by an interfile dependency. But for the same reasons as with TOTAL in ACCOUNTS-PAYABLE, Sarah decides to leave the TOTAL field where it is, at least for the time being. Another note is made of possible difficulty, however.

Now Sarah turns to the problem of incorporating supplier numbers and customer numbers into the data base in Figure 3.11. First supplier numbers. It is clear that SMS can submit many purchase orders to a particular supplier, resulting in many accounts payables records for any particular supplier. Thus there has to be a 1:n relationship between the SUPPLIER conceptual file and the ACCOUNTS-PAYABLE conceptual file, as shown in Figure 3.14. A record of SUPPLIER describes a particular supplier.

In a similar manner, a particular customer can submit many sales orders to SMS, and for each sales order a record in accounts receivable will result. Thus there will be many ACCOUNTS-RECEIVABLES records for any particular customer, so that there has to be a 1:n relationship between the CUSTOMER conceptual file and the ACCOUNTS-RECEIV-ABLE file, as illustrated in Figure 3.14. A record of CUSTOMER describes a particular customer.

These two additional 1:n relationships are depicted in more detail in Figure 3.15. In Figure 3.15a we see that to support the relationship it is necessary to expand ACCOUNTS-RECEIV-ABLE by a single field, namely S# (supplier number), which will serve as a foreign key (or connection field), since S# is the primary key of supplier. Returning now, for a moment, to Figure 3.12, Sarah recalls a difficulty with a lack of information about the supplier number in the INVENTORY-DEBT and INVENTORY-CREDIT files. We now have an S# field in ACCOUNTS-PAYABLE. Is this sufficient?

To test if it is, let us examine a critical function of the data base. In dealing with a customer about selling P66 parts, Tom determines from INVENTORY-DEBIT that there are P66 parts originating from PUR89 and PUR99. It is important for him to know whether these parts come from the same supplier. If they do he may be able to combine the quantities in a delivery to the customer. By checking in the parent ACCOUNTS-PAYABLE records for the two INVENTORY-DEBIT records for the P66

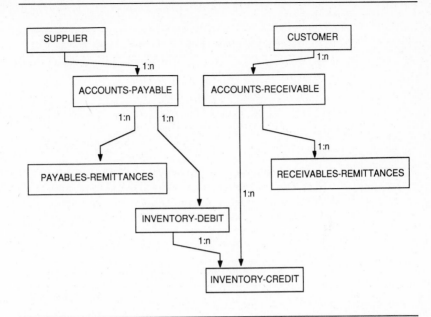

FIGURE 3.14. The data base in Figure 3.11 is still incomplete. We lack information about suppliers and customers, now furnished in the SUPPLIER and CUSTOMER conceptual files. Clearly, for a single supplier there will be many entries in the ACCOUNTS-PAYABLE file, and for a single CUS-TOMER, many entries in ACCOUNTS-RECEIVABLE. This shows that an appropriate cross-reference, or foreign key, or child connection field is missing from both ACCOUNTS-PAYABLE and ACCOUNTS-RECEIVABLE, as displayed in Figures 3.12 and 3.13. This is remedied in Figure 3.15.

parts (identified by PUR89 P66 and PUR99 P66), Tom can extract the supplier numbers for the two part types. This critical information is thus available from the data base.

What about the converse case? Suppose that we want to know the state of inventory of part types P66 from supplier S77. You access the child ACCOUNTS-PAYABLES records for supplier S77. For each of these ACCOUNTS-PAYABLES records you access the child INVENTORY-DEBIT records where the PART-TYPE# value is P66 and sum the QTY values. Call this sum ORIGINAL-SUM. Then for each of these INVENTORY-DEBIT records (for P66 parts) you access the child INVEN-TORY-CREDIT, and sum the QTY values. Call this sum DE-PLETION. Subtract DEPLETION from ORIGINAL-SUM,

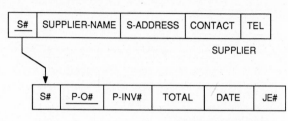

SUPPLIER

ACCOUNTS-PAYABLE

(a) Showing the 1:n relationship between SUPPLIER and ACCOUNTS-PAY-ABLE. The field S# (supplier name) has had to be added to ACCOUNTS-PAYABLE (see Figure 3.12) to support the 1:n relationship. CONTACT holds the name of the contact person at the supplier location.

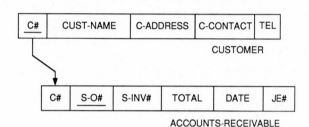

CUSTOMER

ACCOUNTS-RECEIVABLE

(b) Showing the 1:n relationship between CUSTOMER and ACCOUNTS-RECEIVABLE. The field C# (customer number) has had to be added to ACCOUNTS-RECEIVABLE (see Figure 3.13) to support the 1:n relationship. CONTACT holds the name of the contact person at the supplier location.

FIGURE 3.15.

and you have what is currently in stock. Remember that function dictates design.

The detail of the 1:n relationship between CUSTOMER and ACCOUNTS- RECEIVABLE is shown in Figure 3.15b. We see that the earlier version of ACCOUNTS-RECEIVABLE has been expanded to include the foreign key (or child connection field) C#, for customer number. Is this sufficient? We can test with two comprehensive information retrievals. The first is: What customers have bought parts supplied by supplier S33?

Refer to Figure 3.14, and other figures that show requisite detail, as required. Access SUPPLIER record for supplier S33. Access the child ACCOUNTS-PAYABLES records. Access the child INVENTORY-DEBIT records of these payables records, and then all of the child INVENTORY-CREDIT records of these INVENTORY-DEBIT records. Then get the parent ACCOUNTS-RECEIVABLE records of these INVENTORY-DEBIT records. The C# values in these ACCOUNTS-RECEIVABLE records will let us access the required CUSTOMER records.

The second test is to ask: What suppliers have supplied parts, via SMS, to customer C99? Access the C99 CUSTOMER record, its child ACCOUNTS-RECEIVABLES records, and their child INVENTORY-CREDIT records. Then access the parent INVENTORY-DEBIT records of these INVENTORY-CREDIT records, and then the parent ACCOUNTS-PAYABLE of these INVENTORY-DEBIT records. From these ACCOUNTS-PAYABLE records we can extract the required S# values, which can be used to obtain the required SUPPLIER records.

Final Conceptual Data Base Design Steps

The design in Figure 3.14 appears to quite satisfactory (except possibly with regard to the redundant TOTAL values in ACCOUNTS-PAYABLE and ACCOUNTS-RECEIVABLE, and the restriction that a sales order cannot involve a part-type from two distinct suppliers). However, both SUPPLIER and CUS-TOMER conceptual files were used earlier in a different data base involving parts on order and parts committed for sale—that is, the data base in Figure 3.6. Accordingly, the next and final step is the combination of the data base in Figure 3.6 with that in Figure 3.14.

The result is shown in Figure 3.16. As a result of the combination we get two new relationships not considered before. There are the 1:n relationships between PART-TYPE and INVENTORY-DEBIT, and between PART-TYPE and INVENTORY-CREDIT. We can look at these very simply. In both INVENTORY-CREDIT and INVENTORY-DEBIT there is a PART- TYPE# field, and for any given PART-TYPE# value in

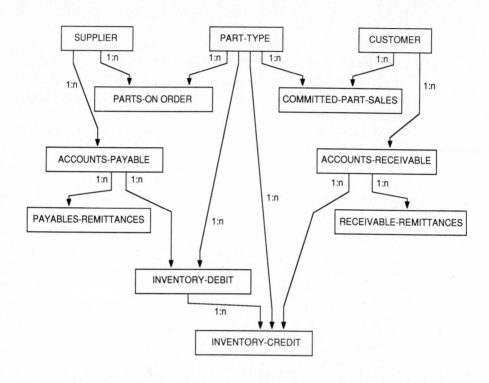

FIGURE 3.16. Showing how the partial data base in Figure 3.6 is combined with the partial data base in Figure 3.14 to form a single data base to cover purchasing and sale or parts. The six conceptual files at the bottom of the diagram are a part of the general ledger files.

these conceptual files there will be many records. Hence, for any record in the conceptual file PART-TYPE there must be many records in both INVENTORY-DEBIT and INVENTORY-CREDIT.

These two new relationships will enable us to respond to such retrieval requests as the following:

(a) Get full descriptions of all part types sold to customer C42.
(b) Get full descriptions of all part types supplied to SMS by supplier S38.

To answer the first of these, you work from CUSTOMER to ACCOUNTS- RECEIVABLE to INVENTORY-CREDIT to PART-TYPE. To answer the second, you work from SUPPLIER to ACCOUNTS-PAYABLE to INVENTORY-DEBIT to PART-TYPE.

The completed data base in Figure 3.16 also allows construction of CONSOLIDATED-INVENTORY, shown in Figure 3.9. We recall that CONSOLIDATED-INVENTORY was generated from PARTS-ON-ORDER, COMMITTED- PART-SALES, INVENTORY DEBIT and INVENTORY-CREDIT, although these four files alone did not contain the information necessary to give the supplier number for a given part type. It should now be clear that this information will come from additional file ACCOUNTS-PAYABLE.

How exactly is CONSOLIDATED-INVENTORY generated? We leave full details to the reader, but essentially we do a sequence of joins as follows:

Start with COMMITTED-PART-SALES and join on PART-TYPE# to PARTS-ON-ORDER, which is then joined, on S#, to ACCOUNTS-PAYABLE, which is then joined, on P-O# to INVENTORY-CREDIT, which is then joined, on the composite P-O# and PART-TYPE# to INVENTORY-CREDIT. The required fields are then extracted, with summations and subtractions required to get the value of QTY-IN-STOCK.

Sarah decides that nothing more can be done with this data base on customers, part types, suppliers, inventory and payables and receivables until the other data base for the remaining general ledger files and the journal is designed, so she looks at that next.

Data Base Design for the Remaining General Ledger Data Base

The design of the data base for the remaining general ledger accounts and the journal is shown in Figure 3.17. Sarah drew on her experience with Lucky Strike Industries with this design, which is essentially the same as the one she designed for LSI. A

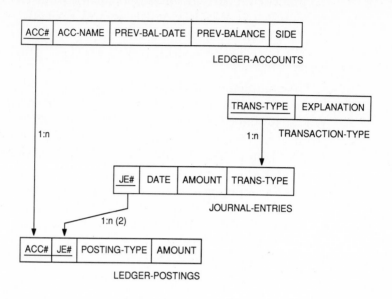

FIGURE 3.17. The design for the data base to handle the journal (JOURNAL-ENTRIES) and all general ledger accounts for the firm, except those to do with accounts receivable, accounts payable, and inventory of components (that is, the six conceptual files at the bottom of Figure 3.16). The design used for the data base above is actually the same one as was used for LSI, Inc. (Chapter 2). The only difference is the field name JE# (journal entry number), which identifies a journal entry, and replaces TRANS#) (transaction number) in the design in Figure 2.7. (The field TRANS-TYPE is still a numeric code that identifies the type of transaction involved, such as payment of rent, purchase of parts, and so on.) Included in the accounts listed in LEDGER-ACCOUNTS will be revenue and expenditure accounts.

minor difference is the use of the field name JE# (journal entry number) instead of the field name TRANS# used in the LSI data base.

The accounts listed in the conceptual file LEDGER-ACCOUNTS do not include the accounts receivable, the accounts payable, any inventory accounts, or any remittances accounts. This is illustrated in Figure 3.18. The records of LEDGER-ACCOUNTS describe such accounts as revenue accounts (very few), expenditure accounts (few), the capital and retained earnings account, and the cash account.

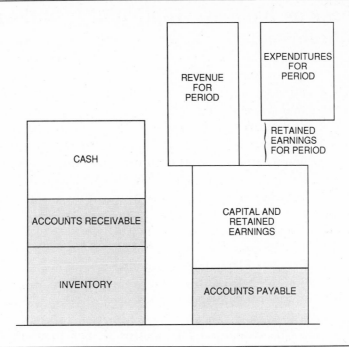

FIGURE 3.18.   Showing the parts of the balance sheet that are the balances of the various general ledger accounts, with the parts shaded being generated from the conceptual files in the purchase/sales data base in Figure 3.16. The parts not shaded are generated from the data base in Figure 3.17, so that the two data bases (Figures 3.16 and 3.17) are needed for both trial balances and generation of balance sheets and income statements.

Whenever there is a transaction, an entry is made in JOUR-NAL-ENTRIES for the amount involved. There will then be one or more records inserted into LEDGER-POSTINGS for the journal entry number involved, and/or appropriate entries made in the conceptual files of the data base for purchase and sale of parts (Figure 3.16). At all times the rules for double-entry bookkeeping have to be followed. Thus, in an attempt at a trial balance, the sum of all credits should equal the sum of all debits. Of course, when we involve the files in the data base for purchase and sale of parts, the intelligence would have to be built into the trial balance application program as to what constituted debits and credits. Nevertheless, all data necessary for a trial balance will be in the two data bases.

Check on Business Applicability of the Proposed Data Bases

When Sarah had finished her design, she did many tests of whether or not the data base was sufficient for all the uses which it would be put, such as trial balances, income statement and balance sheet generation, general ledger posting, generation of shipping documentation (packing slips and invoices), generation of monthly billing statements, generation of views (such as CONSOLIDATED- INVENTORY in Figure 3.9) to aid buying and selling, tracking revenue and costs for individual part types, or part types from individual suppliers, and so on. The data base seemed to be sufficient for all those tasks.

However, Sarah decided that even with a relatively simple firm like SMS, the two data bases together were quite complex, making it difficult for her, or anyone else, to see all the implications of the design. She decided on a walk-through with other professionals.

She explained her desires to her boss, Peter Stone, who agreed to take part in the walk-through. He felt an accountant who was fairly knowledgeable in data base techniques should also be involved, and arranged for Paul Kownter to come. He also arranged for a data-base applications programmer called John Kowed to come too.

At the meeting, Sarah first presented her design, and went through all of the considerations presented in previous pages of this case study. As might be expected, a heated debate arose over Sarah's inclusion of the TOTAL fields in ACCOUNTS-PAYABLE and ACCOUNTS-RECEIVABLE. John Kowed was dead against it. He put forward the usual arguments about standard data base practices and how unnecessary such redundancy was, when it took only a few data base accesses and a few lines of code to get the information from the child INVENTORY-DEBIT and INVENTORY-CREDIT files (respectively).

But Paul Kownter was in favor of keeping the TOTAL fields, arguing on the basis of accounting practice that errors and inconsistency were to be expected and that with the TOTAL fields the existence of such inconsistency could be easily detected. Thus these fields could help detect the errors. Peter

Stone could see that both arguments had merit, as could Sarah. In the end democratic forces prevailed, with a vote of 2 to 1 in favor of keeping the TOTAL fields, with 1 abstention (Peter Stone).

Then Peter brought up the question of how to prevent a sales order with two quantities of the same part type from two different suppliers. The data base design did not prevent the data for such an order being entered. Nobody could see a simple way of redesigning the data base to accomplish this, and after much discussion it was agreed that an integrity constraint preventing insertion of such data to be installed either in the conceptual schema, if the data base system allowed it, or in relevant application programs.

After that the real walk-through began. It consisted of taking each task for which the data base would be used, for example, recording of a purchase, recording of a sale, recording of a commitment to sell, generation of a view, generation of an invoice, and so on, and having one person, in this case Sarah, recount the procedure used for each case and the updates or information retrieval required of the data base, while the others listened and tried to find fault, particularly with respect to the utility of the data base structures.

During the walk-through, no major fault was found, although there was criticism from John Kowed about the existence of two conceptual files, namely INVENTORY-CREDIT and INVENTORY-DEBIT, for tracking inventory. John felt that there was less likelihood of programming errors if there was a single inventory file, in which a record showed the current state of inventory with respect to any part type from a particular purchase order. But here Paul Kownter defended the design as it stood, since the data base gave more than just the current state of affairs with respect to inventory, but all increases and decreases to inventory, as well as associated dollar values, which was just the kind of information that accounting systems record.

After much discussion, it was agreed that the crux of the problem was the multiple uses to which the data base was being put, not only the physical state of inventory from a point of view of purchasing, selling, and maintaining physical volume of inventory, but also the accounting for all matters connected with inventory. It was these two totally divergent uses that were determining Sarah's design—a classic case of function determining design.

The meeting ended with Sarah's basic design being approved.

Final Specifications and Implementation

Before sitting down to draw up the specifications for the application programs that would process the two data bases, there was one last important task for Sarah to carry out. That was the design of the screens to be used at SMS.

With the screens Sarah used the menu approach. A master menu would list all the major operations that could be carried out using the system, for example, the recording of a purchase or a sale, or trial balance, and so on. This master menu would appear on the screen when the user turned on the system. Selection of a master menu item would typically give a submenu, which also lists operations that the system could carry out.

Selection of a submenu item would result in a formatted screen, with blanks to be filled in by the operator. For each such screen, on filling in the blanks, one or more application programs would execute and manipulate the data base, return messages that would also be printed on the screen, and print business documents, such as invoices, monthly billing statements, and so on. In addition, some of the application programs would retrieve information and display the results on the screen in graphic format.

Sarah drew up all the possible screen configurations that would be needed, and drove down to SMS to explain them to the staff there. This took many days, and Sarah soon discovered that she had to redesign many of the screens in order to make the system intelligible and useful to the SMS people. However, in the end there was agreement, and Tom Sayles signed the final part of the contract with Cybertek, authorizing the implementation of the system Sarah had designed. The system was to go on a multi-terminal personal computer, with 60 megabytes of fixed disk storage, and some 4 million bytes of main memory. The data base system was ORACLE, running SQL, which was to be used to minimize the programming effort for the many information retrieval programs.

In the days that followed, with the assistance of John Kowed, Sarah drew up the program specifications for the application programs to manipulate the data base, and, with the use to which the conceptual data base was being put fresh in her mind, she also drew up the storage schema.

The system was implemented and installed by a team directed by John Kowed, with Sarah acting as data base administrator for the project.

When the system was installed, some ten weeks after the project began, it worked as intended. Because Tom's information retrieval needs would become more sophisticated with time, he agreed to hiring a part-time data base administrator to work a few hours a month for SMS. The DBA chosen initially was Sarah, although later an independent consultant filled this role.

In practice it turned out that Sarah's main DBA task was developing views for Tom to manipulate. Tom was an engineer by training, and learning SQL was no problem for him. However, he felt that construction of more complex SQL expressions was hardly worth the effort, given how much time he needed to devote to the nuts and bolts of his business. It was cheaper to have an expert build appropriate views, to which Tom could apply quite simple SQL expressions. In addition, on rare occasions Sarah had to be called in to install an additional index at the storage level. In general, however, performance was more than adequate for the application, so that very little data base turning was required.

Questions

1. Draw up a detailed structure diagram (extended Bachman diagram, entity-relationship diagram, or equivalent) for the parts/sales/purchases/inventory data base in Figure 3.16.
2. Use the DB2 schema language to build a conceptual schema for the two data bases Sarah has designed.
3. Using detailed structure diagrams, show what relationships exist between the two data bases used at SMS.

4. Without actually writing the program code, give details of the procedure, including embedded SQL expressions, if any, for generating the "view" CONSOLIDATED-INVENTORY. Do you think that this view could be specified by means of a single SQL expression? If you think so, produce one.

5. Give details of a procedure for handling receipt of a sales order from a customer. The procedure should include all updates to the data base.

6. Give details of a procedure for generating an invoice for a customer.

7. Give details of a procedure for generating monthly billing statements for each customer. (The statement for a customer shows how much is still owing on each invoiced sales order fulfilled at SMS.)

8. Give details of a procedure for handling updates to the data bases at SMS
   (a) when a purchase order is sent out to a supplier, and
   (b) when the supplier delivers the parts.

9. Give details of the procedure used for handling remittances sent to suppliers by SMS.

10. Give details of the procedure used for handling remittances sent to suppliers by SMS.

11. Give details of the procedure for handling a telephone agreement (no sales order yet received) by Tom with a customer for purchase or parts.

12. Give details of a procedure for a trial balance.

13. Give details of a procedure for generating an income statement.

14. Give details of a procedure for generating a balance sheet for SMS.

15. Argue the pros and cons of including the TOTAL field in the payables and receivables conceptual files.

16. Develop an integrity constraint, possibly using SQL, for the restriction that two different batches of the same part type sold to a customer on a single invoice must be from the same original supplier.

17. Argue the case for the constraint in question 16 being far too restrictive and in need of either revision or elimination.

Use what you know about the operations of SMS in your argument.

18. Redesign the parts/sales/purchases/inventory data base in Figure 3.16, so that all inventory data is in a single conceptual file. Give a detailed structure diagram for your design.

FOUR

General Power, Inc.

General Power is a small manufacturer of electronic subassemblies, particularly that type of subassembly known as a power supply unit. Despite its small size, the company manufactures a surprisingly large number of different types of such products. The reason lies in the very wide diversity of types of power supply units needed by hi-tech equipment manufacturers. Just about every item of electronic equipment, everything ranging from a home tape recorder to a personal computer, requires electrical power of a certain quality (measured in terms of voltage, current, stability, and so on) in order to be able to function. The power supply unit is the device (or subassembly) that supplies such electrical power when the equipment is plugged into an electrical outlet. (The power supply unit converts the power coming from the electrical outlet to the proper voltage and quality to power the electronics of the equipment).

Generally, the construction of a power supply unit is not very difficult, given the proper electronic components and the proper design. A typical power supply unit could have anywhere from ten to thirty components, and can be assembled in less than five minutes. Essentially, General Power, Inc. (or GP) is an assembly operation, for it does not make any of the parts that it uses. However, because of the wide variety of different types of power supply units assembled by GP, a very large variety of different types of parts are used in manufacturing.

Thus, from a physical point of view, GP really consists of a large inventory of parts, an assembly operation using these parts, and a large inventory of finished products. The parts inventory consists of various quantities of a large number of different part types, including everything from circuit boards (into which electronic components are inserted) to integrated circuits. The finished goods inventory consists of quantities of different types of power supply units.

Like Silicon Mountain Supplies, GP is located in Silicon Valley California, near San Jose, and GP is one of Tom Sayles' customers. The owner and founder of GP, Jim Swift, is a good friend of Tom Sayles. However, GP is a much more complex organization than SMS.

Organization of General Power

The layout of GP's manufacturing facility is shown in Figure 4.1. There is a large assembly area for the assembly workers and assembly equipment. To keep labor costs to a minimum, GP uses the most sophisticated equipment in its assembly operation. Many of the power supply units are assembled without being touched by human hands. There are automated assembly machines, whose hoppers are fed by the operator with the required components, and which spew out a fresh power supply unit every few minutes. GP has wizard electronics/computer technicians to keep the automated assembly machines programmed and functional.

The entire manufacturing operation is under the control of Fred Maik, with an assembly staff of up to thirty people, including technicians. Fred has an office from which he can see everything that goes on in the manufacturing process. He runs a very clean and tidy shop, and the workers know better than to leave things lying around or to leave a machine in an untidy state.

There are two inventory areas. One is for finished goods, and the other is for incoming parts inventory. There is a staff of two in finished goods inventory and a staff of four in parts inventory. Finished goods inventory staff also are responsible for shipping and outgoing quality functions, and parts inventory staff are also responsible for receiving and incoming quality functions.

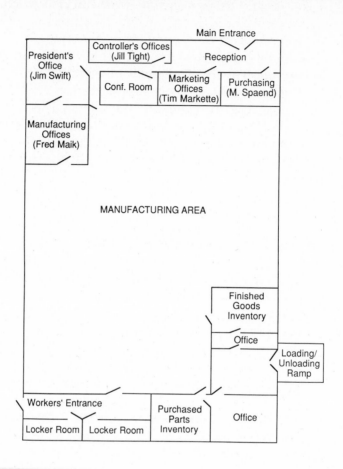

FIGURE 4.1 The layout of the manufacturing and office premises of General Power, Inc., manufacturer of a wide variety of power supply units, by assembling electrical and electronic parts purchased from outside suppliers. There is no engineering function, as all design work is contracted out to engineering firms.

There is no engineering function at GP. New types of power supply units originate with market demand, which is reported by sales people to Jim Swift. In discussion with Fred Maik, Jim decides whether GP should make the new type of unit. If they decide to make a new unit, Fred Maik simply contracts out the design to an engineering firm. Once the design has been determined Fred arranges with the purchasing manager to have the required parts ordered for parts inventory.

The purchasing manager is Mary Spaend, whose job it is to seek out the lowest cost suppliers of quality parts. Typically every part is second-sourced—that is, there has to be atleast two suppliers of that part. In this way, GP ensures that it will always have a supplier for any given part type needed, even if one supplier should be unable to deliver, perhaps because of a strike, or fire, or bankruptcy. To keep quality at high levels, like most equipment manufacturers, GP qualifies its suppliers every few years, which means submitting each supplier to a thorough examination and placing those that pass on a qualified suppliers list. It is engineers on Mary Spaend's staff who look after supplier qualification.

The sales function is under the command of Tim Markette. He has some ten sales people working for him, distributed across the United States, with one in Canada. All finished goods, however, are warehoused at the San Jose plant. A customer will sometimes send an order direct to San Jose. Usually through, the sales order goes first to the local GP sales representative, who transmits the order to San Jose. It is also the marketing department's function to gather information about the demands of the market, with a view to development of new products.

The controller of the firm is Jill Tight, who has a staff of three. The controller's office is responsible for maintaining the firm's books, in particular the journal general ledger. It is responsible for payroll and for documentation relating to purchases (purchase remittances, for example) and sales (invoices, monthly billing statements, and so on).

The firm rents its premises but not the equipment used in manufacturing. There is a relatively large number of expensive pieces of production equipment in the firm, some with original price tags exceeding $350,000, although the average original price might be closer to $20,000. A list of all these assets is kept in the equipment account, together with initial values and depreciated values.

The firm's depreciation policy is very simple. The equipment used is almost all electronic in nature, which rapidly becomes obsolete, and so a simple straight line depreciation schedule of five years is used. That means that each year the current value of each asset is reduced by 20% of the original price.

Computer Systems at General Power

There are two business computer systems in place with General Power: a payroll system and an order entry system, both ultimately under the control of Mary Tight. However, the payroll system is actually run by a firm called Payroll Systems, Inc., for a monthly fee, so that GP escapes having to be concerned about the details. The computer hardware for this system is not even on GP premises.

The order entry system was set up by a service firm called Customer Systems, Inc. This system permits an operator at a terminal at GP to submit sales order information, which is transmitted to Customer Systems' computer and processed. Packing slips, invoices, and monthly billing statements are then printed on a printer in the controller's office at GP as needed.

Although GP has been satisfied with the service from Payroll Systems, the converse is the case with the service from Customer Systems. A major complaint is the high cost of the system. Another complaint is its unreliability, for down time on the system is all too common, and GP has experienced cancellation of orders because of this. And finally there is the lack of integration with other essential data functions, such as information retrieval for marketing and purchasing, and maintaining the general ledger accounts.

Jim Swift is well aware that what the firm needs is an reasonably well integrated set of data bases for the operational data of the firm and associated applications programs. However, he is not prepared to pay for a larger in-house computer staff and computer system in order to have such a system installed. He is not very trusting of computer systems firms, especially Customer Systems, Inc., which, incidentally, has been trying for some time to get a (lucrative, in Jim Swift's opinion) contract from GP for such an integrated system. Jim had approached Payroll Services about such a system, but they, like most well-run firms, had explained that they preferred to stick with what they did best, which was payroll systems.

One day, a potential solution appears. Jim Swift has noticed a marked improvement in the service from Silicon Mountain Supplies in recent months, a service which had always been good, but which recently has become exemplary. It is not long before his old friend Tom Sayles at SMS tells him how pleased he is with the integrated data base system that Cybertek of San Francisco had installed a few months earlier, at a very reasonable initial price and modest maintenance fee. Soon afterwards Jim was in San Francisco explaining his problems to Peter Stone, vice-president in charge of customer development at Cybertek International.

Peter had to point out to Jim Swift that General Power was a much more complex firm than Tom Sayles' Silicon Mountain Supplies, that it could take between three and six months to design and install the kind of system required for the firm's operational data, and perhaps, if unforeseen complications arose, even longer, and that the whole thing would also cost more. Nevertheless, when Cybertek agreed to accept the project, Jim Swift did not hesitate to sign the initial system design contract. (Later, when the system design met with his approval, he would sign an implementation and installation contract.)

When Jim Swift had left, Peter discussed the project with his chief, Joan Braynes, and together they decided that a small system analysis and design team should be formed, made up of Sarah Didget, assisted by Paul Kownter, who was an accountant with a fair knowledge of computers and data bases.

Data Analysis

Sarah and Paul visited GP daily for the better part of two weeks, observing how the existing manual and computer systems worked and interviewing the managers. They did not delve into payroll, as it had been agreed that the payroll function was so specialized that it was best left with Payroll Systems. However, the new system would include order entry, so that the existing order entry system run by Customer Services would be scrapped.

Paul was invaluable to Sarah. Her aim, as always, was to gain an overall understanding of how operational data was recorded and used at the firm. This firm was more complex than any of the others with which she had dealt. The additional complexities were the following:

(a) The firm had a variety of fixed assets, particularly production equipment, which was depreciated, thus involving depreciation accounting.

(b) The firm manufactured its finished goods inventory, which meant specialized accounting.

(c) The firm had both purchased parts and finished goods inventory, which clearly meant more involved inventory accounting.

When all these factors are added to the complexities of accounts receivable, accounts payable, remittances, and so on, with which Sarah was reasonably experienced, you have a level of complexity that overwhelms, and Sarah was somewhat overwhelmed.

It was at this point that Sarah suddenly understood that with any complex firm, there has to be a person well-versed in accounting on a data base design team for most types of data base. There is a great deal to know about computers and data base systems, and to expect the data base specialist to be well-versed in the vast field of accounting as well is just unreasonable. However, the data base specialist needs a knowledge of accounting sufficient to enable him or her to understand the accountant. Conversely, an expert accountant with a knowledge of data bases cannot be expected to design the data bases for a complex firm. There is too much to know about data bases for the accountant to be expert in both fields. Thus the accountant needs the assistance of the data base specialist. Whether the accountant or the data base specialist should be in charge of the design team will obviously depend on the circumstances.

Sarah first had to have the mysteries of depreciation accounting explained to her. After this explanation she was able to draw the balance sheet diagrams in Figure 4.2, which explains the essence of the matter.

Suppose that the firm initially had assets that did not depreciate—that is, gradually lose value through either wear and tear or obsolescence. The situation is shown in the balance sheet in Figure 4.2a, which has been expanded to show the equity increase resulting from greater revenue than expenses over the preceding reporting period (a quarter or a year).

The firm's assets are its cash, accounts receivable, inventory, and fixed assets. (The first three comprise the current assets, which are either cash or other assets that will be converted into cash within a year.) The firm's equity and liabilities are the firm's long term debt (bonds and debentures), its accounts

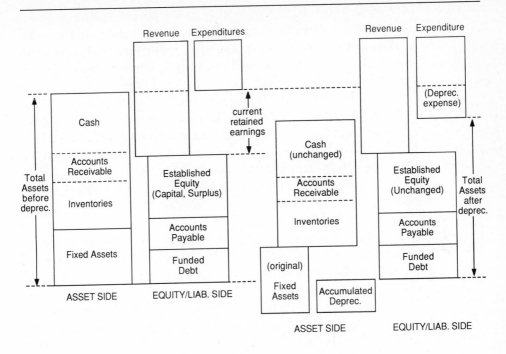

(a) No depreciation taken into account   (b) Depreciation taken into account

FIGURE 4.2. How depreciation is account for. In (a) we have the balance sheet before accounting for depreciation. In (b) we add an accumulated depreciation account to the asset side, so that total fixed assets are obtained by subtracting accumulated depreciation from fixed assets. On the other side, a depreciation expense is added to the expenditures, thus decreasing current retained earnings, and thus profits. Note that neither current assets nor cash is affected by this accounting.

payables (the current liabilities), equity (in the form of initial capital, retained earnings (or surplus) from former periods, and retained earnings for the current period). This current period retained earnings is the difference between revenue and expenditures. And note this important point, the increase in equity due to the current period retained earnings will be matched by an increase in assets, typically cash assets, although any asset increases (for example, accounts receivable) will do. This happens through more cash flowing in with revenue than is flowing out with expenditures.

Now suppose that during this same period we have had a depreciation of the fixed assets—that is, a reduction in the value of these assets. We can manage the recording of this by splitting the fixed assets into fixed assets and accumulated depreciation, as shown in Figure 4.2b. At any instant, the balance of the fixed assets is fixed assets less accumulated depreciation. Thus, if the firm spends cash to acquire new fixed assets, the cash account falls, and the fixed asset account increases. Later, if the fixed assets depreciate, the accumulated depreciation increases, thus reducing total assets; this reduction is matched by a reduction on the equity liability side, which we shall see about shortly. Increases to fixed assets are debits, and increases in accumulated depreciation are credits.

Depreciation is a cost to the firm, so that any increase in depreciation also shows up as an expenditure in the expenditure accounts, which has the effect of reducing the retained earnings for the period, as illustrated in Figure 4.2b (top right). However, the cash on the left increases not by the different of revenue and expenditure, but by the difference of revenue and expenditure before depreciation, because the depreciation expense does not involve the outlay of cash. It might look as if we are getting something for nothing here but the total increase in all assets is just revenue minus expenditures including depreciation. Why? Because initially we decreased the total assets by the depreciation amount—that is, by the increase in the accumulated depreciation account.

In a nutshell, if we enter a depreciation expense, we increase (credit) the accumulated depreciation account and increase (debit) an expenditure account. No other asset account, particularly a current asset account such as cash, is affected. This is so simple that very few non-accountants have ever understood it.

The method of accounting for the parts and finished goods inventory and the manufacturing cost of finished goods can be very complex in an industrial firm. The cost of an item of finished goods, as opposed to its sale price, is the sum of the purchase cost of the parts and raw materials that go into it, plus the direct labor to make it, plus the indirect labor involved, plus the factory overhead, such as electric power and other factory services, plus the direct depreciation of machinery used to make it, plus indirect depreciation of such items as office furniture.

To make matters even more complex. in many firms the process of manufacturing an item can take quite a long time, so that at any instant, there are not only purchased parts and finished goods inventories, but an inventory of work in progress; this work in progress inventory consists of partly finished goods inventory and work in progress, so that data bases are frequently constructed for such management information needs.

Fortunately for Sarah, who had had no experience with data bases for manufacturing data, at GP the manufacturing process and its accounting was as simple as if could be.

First of all, GP divided its payroll into payroll for persons directly involved in the manufacturing process, called manufacturing payroll, and payroll for all others, called staff payroll. Every two weeks, when the work force was paid, Payroll Services, Inc., reported the gross for each of these two payroll categories to GP. These figures were entered into the journal and ledger, and the bill for the gross payroll was paid out of cash to Payroll Services. (Payroll Services was responsible for preparing the workers' paychecks and for looking after all payroll deductions.)

This division of payroll into manufacturing and staff payroll enabled GP to account for the bulk of its direct manufacturing cost in a simple way. There was never any work in progress to account for at GP since the power supply units could be made quite quickly. At the end of each work day there was no work in progress. Units made that day were already in finished goods inventory and accounted for. As we said earlier, GP was run in a very tidy manner. (Many firms are a complex mess, and the management tends to "muddle through"; installing a data base system to clarify things for management with such firms tends to make the mess even more incomprehensible.)

The progress of purchased parts inventory through the production process to finished goods inventory, and its accounting, is illustrated in Figure 4.3. To keep the illustration simple, we assume for the moment that the firm has no fixed assets and no long term debt. In Figure 4.3a we show the firm at the start of a day in which no power supply units are sold, and no parts are purchased. Therefore, we have only increases in finished goods inventory to concern us. Let us assume also that the workers were paid the previous day. At the end of the day there will be

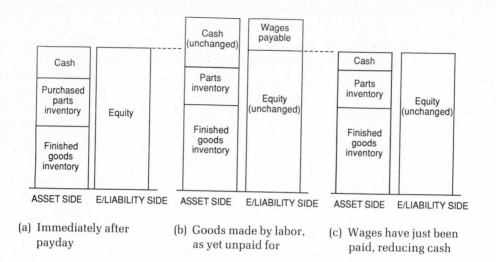

FIGURE 4.3 diagrams, from left to right:

(a) Immediately after payday — Asset side: Cash, Purchased parts inventory, Finished goods inventory; E/Liability side: Equity

(b) Goods made by labor, as yet unpaid for — Asset side: Cash (unchanged), Parts inventory, Finished goods inventory; E/Liability side: Wages payable, Equity (unchanged)

(c) Wages have just been paid, reducing cash — Asset side: Cash, Parts inventory, Finished goods inventory; E/Liability side: Equity (unchanged)

FIGURE 4.3.   Showing how accounting for the manufacturing operation is handled, for the simplest case. During manufacturing, finished goods increases as purchased parts decrease, being used up. The increase in recorded cost of finished goods is greater than the decrease in recorded cost of purchased parts, because to the cost of the direct labor used in manufacturing, accounted for in wages payable. When wages are actually paid, wages payable falls to zero, and the cash (from which wages are paid) falls by an equal amount.

fewer parts in purchased parts inventory and more power supply units in finished goods inventory, as illustrated in Figure 4.3b. However, the increase in finished goods inventory value will be greater than the decrease in purchased parts inventory value because of the cost of direct labor to convert the parts to finished goods.

Thus the manufacturing process causes the total assets to increase on any given day. Does this mean that equity, on the right, increases by an equivalent amount? No. The extra value imparted to the finished goods by manufacturing comes from the cost of the labor, which has not yet been paid for and will not be paid for until the next payday. Accordingly, a liability for wages has been incurred, and this shows up on the right as wages payable (which, along with accounts payable), is part of current liabilities, or current debt). As each day passes, the wages payables account will increase, with corresponding additions to finished goods, until payday arrives, when the wages payable falls to zero, and there is a corresponding drop in cash (used to pay the wages), as is illustrated in Figure 4.3c.

At the end of each day, an amount is entered in wages payable. Thus we have an addition to, or increase in, finished goods inventory value (at cost) by the total of the cost of the parts and the cost of the direct labor entered into wages payable. But how is this cost of labor allocated to each individual power supply unit? The different types of unit will require different amounts of direct labor to make (not to mention indirect costs).

Tracking the cost of making different kinds of parts involves complex accounting systems that are necessary in most manufacturing concerns. However, in the case of GP, things are simpler. Management has found that it takes more or less the same amount of direct labor for each type of unit. The extra effort to determine exactly how much labor is used for each type of unit is uneconomic. So, at the end of each day, to get the labor cost of each unit, the amount of direct labor used is divided by the number of units of all types manufactured. This figure is then used to describe the value of the units (at cost) in finished goods inventory. Management knows that because of direct costs, the cost of a unit in finished goods inventory is actually somewhat higher than the figure stated in the firm's books. But this is as close as they can come without a great increase in accounting system complexity.

Sarah found that the accounting for sales was similar to the case with Silicon Mountain Supplies, except that this time the sales were coming out of finished goods inventory, and the purchase orders were coming in from sales people spread out over the country.

How GP accounted for sale of power units is illustrated in Figure 4.4, where we once again ignore fixed assets. In Figure 4.4a we show the balance sheet initially. When units are sold, the sale takes place on credit. The finished goods inventory decreases by the cost of the goods sold, as shown in Figure 4.4b, and the expenditure account increases by the same amount. This keeps the balance sheet balanced. (It also demonstrates that the firm has to know what it costs to make a particular type of unit. How this is done was explained above.) At the same

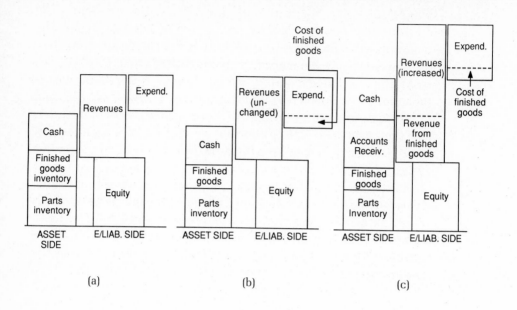

(a)   **(b)**   **(c)**

FIGURE 4.4. Showing the accounting for sale of finished goods. In (b) finished goods are sold, and the expenditure account increases by the cost (not sale price) of goods. Then, in (c), revenue is increased by sale price (not cost) of finished goods, and the asset side has an equal amount entered in account receivable, if the goods are sold on credit, otherwise the amount is entered in cash. The net result is a profit—that is, increase in retained earnings (equity) by the difference between sale price and cost of goods, or an increase in assets by this same profit. Thus the profit from manufacturing is entered into the ledger only when the goods are sold. Before that they are carried at cost.

time, as illustrated in Figure 4.4c, the revenue account increases by the sum received for the goods (not the cost of the goods), and this is balanced by an increase in accounts receivable. The net result is an increase in the firm's equity—that is, a profit for the firm.

In the course of time, the accounts receivable amount is eliminated by one or more remittances from the customer, with a corresponding increase in cash.

Data Base Design

As soon as Sarah was clear about how the firm functioned, both in terms of the physical system and the accounting system, she began to consider the outlines of the design for the data base or data bases needed. She first drew up a formal data/process matrix, listing all the kinds of data involved along one side of the matrix and all the processes in which the data was used along the other. At the same time she used the list of types of data as a preliminary data dictionary.

Sarah did not have to juggle the data/processing matrix much in order to come up with the natural groupings of the data. She could see that there were three:

(a) Data connected with purchase, inventory, and accounting for the parts used in manufacturing.
(b) Data connected with the sale, inventory, and accounting for the power supply units sold by the firm.
(c) Data connected with the journal and all other general ledger accounts. (Payroll data is not involved, except for gross payroll figures being entered into the journal and certain general ledger accounts.)

However, Sarah wondered if there should not be just two data bases, with the integration of purchasing, all inventory, and sales—that is, something along the lines of the data bases designed for Silicon Mountain Suppliers. (Readers should be familiar with that case (Chapter 3) before delving into this case.) After all, the businesses were essentially similar, the major differences being the manufacturing leading to finished goods inventory and the depreciation of fixed assets.

She discussed the problem with Paul Kownter. Although he had been invaluable in explaining the accounting ins and outs of General Power, he was a bit hazy about the finer points of data base design, especially when it involved a decision about three data bases versus two. In the end Sarah had to think the thing through for herself. But when she had done so, she was quite clear about what to do.

It was really simple. In the case of Silicon Mountain Supplies, the data about sales was intimately connected with the data about purchases. When the parts were purchased they went into inventory (INVENTORY-DEBIT), and came out of inventory again when sold (as recorded in INVENTORY-CREDIT). Not so with General Power. Parts go into inventory due to purchases, but sales cause power supply units to come out of finished goods inventory. Indeed, suppose that there was a strike at GP with no manufacturing. If finished goods inventory had been well stocked before the strike, GP could go on selling power supply units even though nothing was coming out of purchased parts inventory to go into the manufacturing process.

Purchased parts inventory and finished goods inventory were linked only through the manufacturing process. Thus it was clear that parts purchasing data was linked to manufacturing data, which was in turn was linked to sales data. But there was no direct link between purchasing and sales data—only an indirect link via manufacturing.

This realization caused Sarah to wonder if there really should be three data bases here: a purchasing data base, a manufacturing data base, and a sales data base. She decided to go back to GP and talk with Fred Maik, the manufacturing manager. What he told he convinced her that in this particular case the manufacturing process was so simple that no manufacturing data base was necessary.

In an answer to a question from Sarah about whether it was likely that someone at GP would have to trace the parts used in a particular power supply unit back through manufacturing to parts inventory and the ultimate supplier of the parts, Fred told her that such an operation was highly unlikely, and that if it ever were necessary the tracing from power supply unit to part types would not be done via any recorded data: The parts used in making a power supply unit are simply attached to a circuit board, with the part identification numbers easily visible. Once a would-be investigator, for example, in the case of a failure investigation, had the part type numbers from the failed unit, he or she could use the purchasing and parts inventory data to find out all about the history of the parts used in that unit. This indicated that a data base linking finished goods and incoming parts was not necessary.

However, Sarah still had doubts and pressed further. "How," she asked, "do your people know how to make a given type of power supply unit, without some documentation as to the parts needed?" Fred replied that there was a blueprint and other design information for each type of unit manufactured. These were kept by the engineering firms that designed the units. However, the information about exactly how to make a particular type of unit was programmed into the computer-controlled assembly machines; if you wanted ZP55 type units, you just entered that code at the machine's keyboard, and the machine would do the rest.

Fred took Sarah over to a machine that was making XL42 units. It was an impressive machine, and in its hoppers there was a wide variety of part types and even circuit boards. To make an XL42 unit, the machine first spat out a circuit board and gripped it firmly; then it literally began shooting parts into the circuit board, like a machine gun, and just as loudly. Finally the machine attached the part type number and a batch number to the circuit board, before ejecting the finished unit. Then it was off to the next unit. Half way through making this unit the machine ran out of P56 part types. It stopped and gave a loud beep-beep, and printed on its display screen:

Load P56 part types in hopper No. 15.

The operator promptly loaded the required part types, and the machine continued as before. Sarah was convinced, and thanked Fred for his time. As she was leaving, curiosity got the better of her, and she asked Fred if anyone at GP actually understood how the power supply units worked. "Nobody", said Fred, "We just make them."

It was now clear to Sarah that in a more complex manufacturing operation, involving considerable manufacturing time and both manual and machine operation, a manufacturing data base would be very useful, and probably necessary, and would involve bill-of-materials data base structures and recursive relationships. In addition, such a data base would enable anyone to trace backwards from a manufactured unit to its component parts and subassemblies. However, in this case at GP none of this was necessary, and the link between finished goods and incoming parts could be ignored.

Sarah decided to start with a rough initial design for the purchasing data base. She began by using an entity-relationship diagram, but decided that since she had a fair idea already of the structure of this data base (from her experience with Silicon Mountain Supplies) she would not worry about the fields in the individual conceptual files. Thus, she used ordinary Bachman diagrams for her preliminary designs. The preliminary purchasing data base is shown in Figure 4.5a.

We can see that the conceptual files and the relationships used in the design are precisely those used in the purchasing/ inventory data base for part types at Silicon Mountain Supplies. There are two files for inventory: one for increases in inventory, called P-INVENTORY-DEBIT, and the other for decreases to inventory, and called P-INVENTORY-CREDIT. A record of P-INVENTORY-DEBIT will give the part type number, the quantity of parts, the unit cost, and the number of the purchase order with which the parts were ordered. An ACCOUNTS- PAYABLE record is identified by the purchase order number and records a sum payable on that purchase order (see Figure 3.12). There is thus a 1:n relationship between ACCOUNTS-PAYABLE and P-INVENTORY-DEBIT.

A record of P-INVENTORY-CREDIT describes a quantity of parts removed from inventory to go into manufacturing. Parts are taken out of inventory in batches, each with a unique batch number, and a record of P-INVENTORY-CREDIT will have fields like:

P-O# PART-TYPE# BATCH# DATE QTY JE#

where P-O# is the number of the purchase order with which the parts in the batch were ordered from the supplier originally. Sarah has determined that a batch of parts always has parts (a) of the same type, and (b) that come from a single supplier. Thus the batch number requirement means that the P-INVENTORY-CREDIT file is going to differ slightly from its counterpart (INVENTORY-CREDIT) in the Silicon Mountain Supplies data base. Without going into details, the other files of the data base, namely SUPPLIER and PAYABLES-REMITTANCES, are expected to be essentially the same as with SMS.

In Figure 4.5b we have a preliminary design for the purchasing data base. Sarah has modified the corresponding data struc-

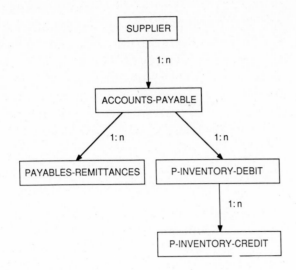

(a) Purchasing data base

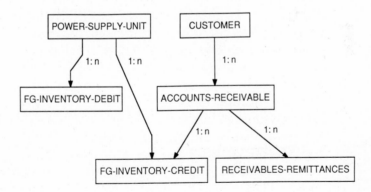

(b) Sales data base

FIGURE 4.5. Showing the natural division between the data bases for purchasing and sales. The purchasing data base has much the same structure as the corresponding part of the data base for Silicon Mountain supplies; parts inventory items are identified partly by part-type number. The purchasing data base has some similarity with the Silicon Mountain Supplies data base; finished goods inventory items are partly identified by unit-type number.

ture in the SMS data base to come up with this structure. The CUSTOMER, ACCOUNTS- RECEIVABLES, and RECEIV-ABLES-REMITTANCES are essentially as in the SMS case. The different lies in the remaining conceptual files.

A record for FG-INVENTORY-DEBIT describes an increase in the inventory of a particular type of power supply unit. Units are fed into finished goods inventory in batches, a batch being the quantity of a given part type made during a day. Thus a record of FG-INVENTORY- DEBIT will have fields like:

UNIT-BATCH#   UNIT#   QTY   DATE   JE#

Finished goods inventory should have information about the cost of finished goods, but Sarah is quite sure that a UNIT-COST field cannot go in FG-INVENTORY-DEBIT, since it would be functionally dependent on UNIT# (assuming costs tend not to change from batch to batch), and not on the primary key field UNIT-BATCH#. The field UNIT-COST, giving the cost of both the parts and the labor that goes into making a unit, must be held in a record describing that unit, thought Sarah—that is, in a record of POWER-SUPPLY-UNIT. [This reasoning can be seriously criticized, however.]

A record of POWER-SUPPLY-UNIT describes an individual type of power-supply unit, with UNIT# as the primary key field, and a large number of fields describing technical aspects of the unit. In addition there is the field UNIT-COST, the value for which is entered by the controller's staff. Clearly there will be a 1:n relationship between POWER-SUPPLY-UNIT and FG-INVENTORY-DEBIT.

A record of the finished goods inventory file FG-INVENTORY-CREDIT records each decrease in inventory of finished units due to a sales order. A record will list the unit identification number (UNIT#), the quantity of units of that type sold, the unit sale (not cost) price, and the sales order number, that is, the fields:

UNIT#S-O#   QTY   UNIT-SALE-PRICE

The cost of the units sold can be obtained from the parent POWER-SUPPLY-UNIT records, and the date, and journal number for the transaction can be obtained from the parent ACCOUNTS-RECEIVABLE record.

Preliminary Design Review

Sarah now reviews the design in terms of how the firm functions, to see if her initial design models the firm correctly. Suppose that the firm issues a purchase order for several different types of parts from a certain supplier. When the parts arrive an entry is made in the journal. A record describing the purchase order is now placed in ACCOUNTS-PAYABLE, and for each line of the purchase order, a record is inserted into P-INVENTORY-DEBIT. Thus the state of inventory and its value are maintained.

Next morning, several batches of different parts are taken out of inventory into manufacturing. For each part and for each original purchase order involved, a record is inserted into P-INVENTORY-CREDIT, following an entry in the journal, Once more the state of parts inventory is properly recorded.

That evening several batches of power-supply units are moved from manufacturing into finished goods inventory. For each batch a record is inserted into FG-INVENTORY-DEBIT detailing the type of unit and quantity involved, following an entry in the journal. Finished goods inventory is thus properly maintained, for we can get the value of the inventory (at cost) by using the quantity (QTY) fields from PG- INVENTORY-DEBIT and the unit-cost from the parent POWER-SUPPLY-UNIT records.

Next day, a sales order is filled for several different types of power-supply unit. An entry goes into the journal for the sum involved. A record also goes into ACCOUNTS-RECEIVABLES giving at least the sales order number, the customer responsible for the order, the journal entry number, the invoice number, and the date. For each line- item on the sales order, a record will be inserted into FG-INVENTORY- CREDIT, recording the type of unit, quantity, and the unit sale price. Thus finished goods inventory is properly maintained. Using both FG-INVENTORY-CREDIT and FG-INVENTORY-DEBIT, as well as the unit cost data in POWER-SUPPLY-UNIT, we can get the total quantity and manufacturing cost for each type of unit in inventory.

Extension of the Basic Data Base Designs

Satisfied that she had arrived at the essential cores of her data bases for purchases and sales, Sarah went on to extend these data bases and incorporate other more peripheral, but still very essential, conceptual files.

In Figure 4.6 we have the extension of the purchasing data base. A conceptual file PART-TYPE has been added, each of whose records describes a part type. A conceptual file PARTS-ON-ORDER has also been added. A record of this file lists a part type number, quantity ordered, unit price, date ordered, and purchase order number, and supplier, for orders issued to a supplier when the parts have yet to be delivered. Finally there is a file called QUALIFICATION. A supplier has to undergo a rigorous test of capability of manufacture of a given

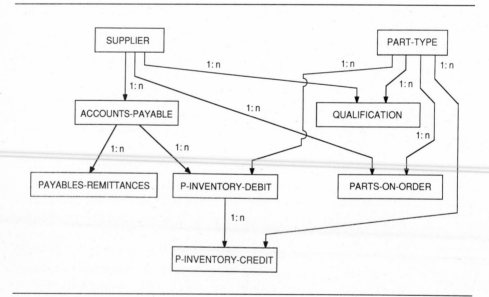

FIGURE 4.6. Expansion of the purchasing data base. Each record in P-INVENTORY-DEBIT describes a quantity of a part type added to inventory. Each part type is described in PART-TYPE (with primary key PART-TYPE#). A supplier is qualified for each type of part, and a record in QUALIFICA-TION lists a supplier, a part type, date of initial qualification and date of qualification expiry. A record of PARTS-ON- ORDER essentially gives the quantity of a part-type on order, with order number and date of order.

type of part. If a supplier passes, the supplier is regarded as qualified to supply that part for a certain period, after one or two years, at the end of which period the supplier might have to submit to a further test for qualification renewal. A record of QUALIFICATION lists supplier, part type, and dates of initial qualification, and expiry. For every part type listed in PART-TYPE it was a requirement that there should be at least two qualified suppliers. Sarah made a note that there would have to be an application program that could check for this and that could warn manufacturing management when there was only one qualified supplier for a part type.

An expansion of the sales data base in shown in Figure 4.7. We have added a conceptual file SALESPERSON, each record

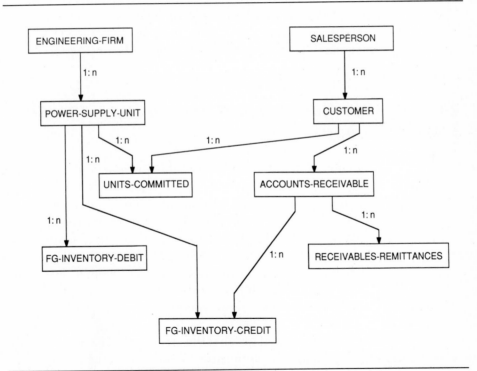

FIGURE 4.7. Expansion of the sales data base. POWER-SUPPLY-UNIT describes the firms products (one record per product type). A record of ENGINEERING-FIRM describes an engineering firm that designed one or more product types. A record of UNITS-COMMITTED describes a quantity of units that have been committed for sale to a customer.

of which describes a sales person. Each customer will be in the sales territory of some sales person, so that there will be a 1:n relationship between SALESPERSON and CUSTOMER. We have also added a file called UNITS-COMMITTED. When an order comes in over the telephone, without any hard-copy documentation, it is not placed on hold, but as with SMS, for each unit type ordered a record is placed in UNITS-COMMITTED, giving the quantity involved. The true inventory from a marketing standpoint (but not an accounting standpoint) is then the sum of the number of units physically in finished goods inventory (obtainable form FG-INVENTORY-DEBIT and FG-INVENTORY-CREDIT) less the number committed for sale.

Finally the conceptual file ENGINEERING-FIRM lists the engineering firms that can be, and have been, used to design the power-supply units. There will be a 1:n relationship between ENGINEERING-FIRM and POWER-SUPPLY, and to support this relationship there will be a field in POWER-SUPPLY to identify the engineering firm that designed a unit type.

Data Base for Journal and Remaining General Ledger Accounts

The design of the data base for the journal and remaining general ledger accounts was simple enough for Sarah. She proposed using the design for the corresponding data base for SMS, shown again in Figure 4.8. The accounts listed in LEDGER-ACCOUNTS would include the usual accounts for revenue, expenditures, cash, and so on. However, with General Power some additional accounts would be needed. For example, there was the matter of depreciation accounting, and the business of wages payable in accounting for cost of manufactured units.

First Sarah checked to see if the structure in Figure 4.8 could handle depreciation accounting. There had to be accounts for fixed assets, accounts for accumulated depreciation, and expense accounts for depreciation expenses. Consider the three accounts for an item of fixed assets, for example, a machine. When the machine is purchased for $250,000 there will be an entry in the journal. This will later be posted to the

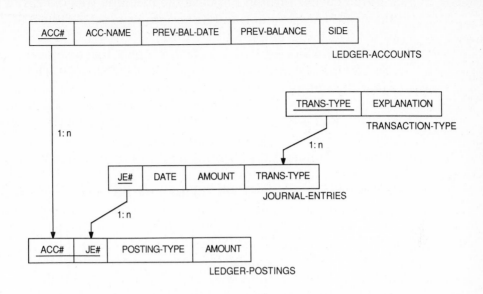

FIGURE 4.8. Preliminary data base for the general ledger accounts for General Power, Inc., and for journal entries. Parts and finished goods inventory accounts, accounts receivable and payable, and remittances accounts are not included here, but are to be found in the data bases in Figures 4.6 and 4.7. This data base has the same structure as the one used for Silicon Mountain Supplies. For details on how depreciation is handled, and also the manufacturing cost of finished goods, see the explanations in the text. Because of difficulties with depreciation, the modified version of this data base in Figure 4.9 is much better.

general ledger. A debit record for $250,000 will be inserted into LEDGER-POSTINGS for the fixed assets account for this machine, and a credit record of $250,000 will be inserted into cash.

Suppose now that the machine depreciates $50,000 each year or $12,500 per quarter. At the end of the quarter a credit record for $12,500 will be inserted into the account for accumulated depreciation for this machine, and a balancing debit record will be inserted into the depreciation expense account for this machine. Also an entry for this amount will be made in the journal. The above updates are all possible with the data base in Figure 4.8.

Sarah checks further. Suppose the machine was the ZAP80 (the ACC-NAME value), and its account was A2345 (the ACC# value). The initial entry in LEDGER-POSTINGS under account A2345 would be a debit of $250,000. Suppose that a new attachment for the machine is purchased at a cost of $50,000. That too would be entered into LEDGER-POSTINGS under account A2345 as a debit; later if a part of the machine was sold for $25,000, that too would to into LEDGER-POSTINGS under A2345 as a credit. Thus the sum of the entries in LEDGER-POSTINGS under A2345 would give the undepreciated value of the machine.

To get the depreciated value of machine ZAP80, the entries in its accumulated depreciation account would have to be added and subtracted from the balance of A2345. Thus the two sets of entries in LEDGER- POSTING will be needed to get the depreciated value of ZAP80, those for undepreciated value in A2345, and those in the accumulated depreciation account. But how are these two sets related? Where is the cross-referencing? Sarah is suddenly startled. She has uncovered a fundamental design flaw.

Fortunately, the solution is very simple and comes from recognizing that the account A2345 for ZAP80 is superior to the account (A7789) for ZAP80's depreciation. Accordingly, the solution is the account number field (P-ACC#) in LEDGER-ACCOUNTS, as shown in Figure 4.9. Essentially we are bringing a recursive 1:n relationship into LEDGER-ACCOUNTS, although since we need it only for depreciation in this case, the recursive aspect is very minimal.

Let us see how this works. Suppose that we have asset account A2345 for the ZAP80 machine, and that the depreciation account for this machine is A7789. First of all in LEDGER-ACCOUNTS we will have the record for the asset account A2345, with A2345 as the primary key value; the P-ACC# for this record will be empty. We will also have a record with primary key A7789 for the accumulated depreciation account for the ZAP80 machine; however, in this record, the account number of the superior account—that is, the asset account number A2345—will be in the P-ACC# field.

Thus, if we have found a balance for all asset account A2345 entries (from LEDGER-POSTINGS), to get the balance of any

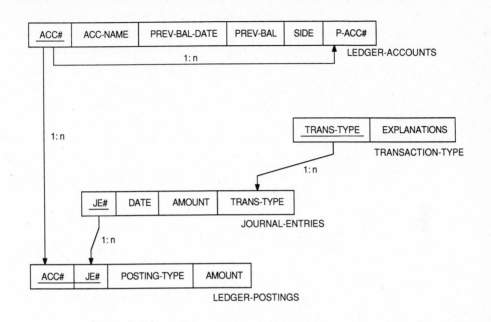

FIGURE 4.9. Modified version of the data base in Figure 4.8. There is one simple change, which produces a very large effect. The addition of the field P-ACC# to LEDGER-ACCOUNTS gives that conceptual file a recursive 1:n relationship, necessary to handle accounts that are subsidiary to other accounts—in this case, accumulated depreciation accounts that are subsidiary to asset accounts. If a record is describing a depreciation account A7789 (ACC# key field value A7789), then the P-ACC# field will contain the account number for the asset which is being depreciated (A2345). There will also be a record in LEDGER-ACCOUNTS with ACC# key field value A2345.

subsidiary account, in this case only the one depreciation account, we extract from LEDGER-ACCOUNTS that record with P-ACC# equal to A2345. From the ACC# value in this record we get the account number of the depreciation account and use it with LEDGER-POSTINGS to get the balance. This will enable us to get the depreciated value of the ZAP80 by subtracting the two balances (and taking any PREV-BAL values in LEDGER-ACCOUNTS into consideration).

Essentially, what all this means is that if the asset account number is A2345 for the ZAP80 machine, then the full account number for the subsidiary depreciation account is really A2345 A7789. This type of extended account number is common in accounting where we have cascades of subsidiary accounts. For example, a capital asset account might have number 2345, but a subsidiary manufacturing asset might have the number 2345 1234; going further down the cascade, a particular manufacturing machine might have account number 2345 1234 6789, and so on.

Readers might wonder why we did not just use full account number fields instead of ACC#, that is, a primary key field in LEDGER- ACCOUNTS like A1 A2 A3 A4, which is a composite made up of superior account number A1, subsidiary account number A2, and so on. The answer is that if you do that, which is what accountants do, you will need such a composite as a subkey in LEDGER-POSTINGS as well, which can cause inconsistency. The single alteration to LEDGER-ACCOUNTS in Figure 4.9 is much simpler and is quite sufficient. To understand the full implications of this you have to be familiar with recursive 1:n relationships, however.

As a final check of the data base in Figure 4.9, Sarah now looks at wages payable. As we saw earlier the wages payable account is used to track the direct cost of manufacturing power supply. At the end of a day an entry will be made in FG-INVENTORY-DEBIT to reflect manufacture of power-supply units and thus the increased value (at cost) of finished goods inventory. A balancing entry is needed for the cost of the labor, which has not yet been paid for. This will go into the account called wages payable, which is listed in LEDGER-ACCOUNTS in Figure 4.9. See also Figure 4.3. To record a wages payable entry, a record is placed in JOURNAL-ENTRIES, and later a record in LEDGER- POSTINGS. Thus the data base in Figure 4.9 is adequate for this purpose.

A Fundamental Difficulty

Next day Paul Kownter comes to see Sarah and tells her that he has very carefully analyzed her three data bases and uncovered a fundamental flaw. Fortunately, in this case the flaw can be lived with, if taken account of in trial balance application programs. Sarah is somewhat shocked, for she had thought that her design was flawless.

Paul explains that the problem has to do with the accounting for manufacturing costs, which is a very difficult area, even for accountants. The problem is that even if every entry required by double entry bookkeeping is made without errors of any kind, on the trial balance the debits will not equal credits. We shall not get into the explanation here. However, Sarah is even more shocked by the sheer subtlety of the error once she understood it. Nevertheless, she learned a great deal from it and began to appreciate what Paul Kownter had said many times: Accounting is a very tricky subject, and when you mix accounting up with operational data bases, even in the case of a firm of minor complexity, subtle errors are very hard to avoid.

The practical solution to the difficulty is an additional account, called parts-in-manufacturing, to be listed in LEDGER-ACCOUNTS. No change to the data base structure is needed. To get the accounts to balance (debits equal credits) a record has to be inserted in LEDGER-POSTINGS for the account parts-in-manufacturing just before a trial balance, which typically would be carried out at a time when manufacturing had ceased for the day, all newly produced units had been transferred to inventory, and appropriate entries made in all accounts. The funds entered into the parts-in-manufacturing account would include an estimate of the value of the parts left in the hoppers of the machines when manufacturing ceased. There will always be some parts left in the hoppers, although their value is not expected to be high. The lack of a value for these parts in the ledger is a good part of the reason why the books will not balance. (Another reason has to do with direct labor approximations, as explained in the appendix.) Since the value of these parts in the machine hoppers must necessarily be an estimate, at trial balance time this value will be adjusted to get the books to balance.

Sequel

We cut short the rest of our story of the development of data bases and associated applications software for General Power.

The usual sequence of activities was followed. A team at Cybertek walked through the data bases for every operation that was required, checking updating, information retrieval, and business document generation. As a result of the walk-through, some minor improvements were made to Sarah's design. Then terminal locations were decided, GP approval was obtained for screen designs, a computer was selected, the application software was implemented, a data base administrator was hired by GP (under the command of the controller), the data bases were loaded, and the system gotten up and running. There were glitches, headaches, and some delays, but also some pleasant surprises, and in the end it all worked.

The project also marked the end of a career stage with smaller companies for Sarah, where the company was sufficiently small and simple that it was possible to get a bird's eye view, in detail, of how the whole thing worked. Her later projects involved partially isolated data bases in large complex organizations. Unlike the cases with small companies, where everything usually functioned under the watchful eyes of their owner-founders, in the large organizations things often functioned according to the norms of bureaucracy.

In time Sarah learned to survive in the bureaucratic jungle. And just as she had to be forced to develop her accounting skills when dealing with small firms, when dealing with large firms she was forced to develop skills in both team work and diplomacy. In addition, as she had learned form her projects with small firms, she always tried to understand how her project fitted into the big picture for the company.

In the remaining cases in this book, we are dealing with data bases for large organizations. Sarah Didjet is involved in these projects, and her work on these and other large projects helped her understand that to be a successful data base analyst and designer, you need four basic skills—or at least, these four skills should be available in the design team:

(a) data base skills,
(b) accounting skills,
(c) diplomacy/negotiation skills
(d) the imaginative skills necessary to grasp the big picture.

Sarah did develop all of these skills to some extent, although her character type did not allow her to be really good in the diplomacy/negotiation area. Nevertheless, she did well, and as we shall see, where diplomacy/negotiation skills were really critical to a project, other team members usually provided this expertise.

Appendix: *Balance Problems with the GP Data Bases*

Each morning, parts worth $X come out of inventory to go into manufacturing. Each evening units worth $Y + $W come out of manufacturing to go into finished goods inventory. If all the parts that went into manufacturing were used up during the day, and the machine hoppers were empty in the evening, then X = Y. Thus a parts inventory credit of $X, is matched by a finished goods inventory debit of $X + $W, and a wages payable credit of $W. Thus the posting operations match debits and credits. However, where X ≠ Y, there is a slight mismatch, which will be negative some days and positive on other days. On average these differences cancel out, although on any given evening, if a trial balance is attempted, there will be a credit/debit mismatch approximately equal to the value of the parts left in the hoppers at the time the books are closed. The mismatch is not exactly equal to the value of the parts in the hoppers because of the averaging effect, but also for the fundamental reason that follows.

The controller at GP has no way of knowing exactly the cost of the parts that went into a particular power supply unit. You might think that all he has to do is identify the parts in the assembly and add up their costs. However, it is not so simple. It is hard to keep track of parts once they go into manufacturing. Suppose a unit uses two P56 parts. Those two parts could have come to GP from two different suppliers, at two different prices, or at the same price, or they could have come from the same supplier in the same purchase order, or from the same supplier with different orders at different prices. No record is kept of exactly which parts from which purchase order at which price go into a given unit. And parts costs fluctuate, depending on market conditions—boom or slump, and so on.

Thus the controller's office never knows exactly what the parts in a given unit have cost, although, based on past experience, a very close estimate is possible. It will be this estimate that is used when entering the total cost of units manufactured during any day (plus the cost of labor). These will thus be a small error. On average, over a period of months, these small errors will cancel each other out, although on any given day, there will be a resulting small mismatch between total debits and total credits. At trial balance time, this small mismatch is covered by the entry for the value of parts in manufacturing.

There is another related difficulty that has to do with the cost of finished goods. We have seen that the cost of direct labor has to be included in the value (at cost) of each type of unit. This direct labor cost will clearly vary from day to day and from batch and batch, even for the same kind of unit, and it will certainly vary from one unit type to another. The controller's office simply uses the average value of the labor applied to all units. To get the value of the labor in a unit, divide the total factory labor cost that day by the total number of units produced.

The obvious result of this method is that XL42 units made one day will have a slightly different labor costs as compared with XL42 units made another day. However, readers should be able to see that this procedure will result in the debit for the labor content of units going into finished goods inventory will be exactly matched by the credit for labor going into wages payable. Thus it does not result in a mismatch of credits and debits, as does the estimate used for the value of parts used in finished units.

A corollary to these very fine details is that to do the job properly an accounting system has to be set up to track parts through manufacturing to finished product, taking into account the direct and indirect labor used and also other factory overhead. Such accounting systems are common with more complex manufacturing operations. Associated with such an accounting system nowadays will be a manufacturing data base, which will enable management to know exactly what parts have gone where and exactly what it costs at any given time to manufacture a given product type.

Such manufacturing accounting systems and associated data bases and software tend to reflect the manufacturing process. However, they also tend to be complex, and the data bases frequently involve recursive structures. Unfortunately, we do not have the space in this case book to cover an example thoroughly. Details of the accounting systems involved can be found in any standard accounting text.

Questions

1. Give full details of all fields in the conceptual files for the data base for purchasing in Figure 4.6. Draw either an entity- relationship or extended Bachman diagram.
2. Give full details of the fields in the conceptual files for the sales data base in Figure 4.7. Draw either an entity-relationship or extended Bachman diagram for the data base.
3. Give a list of all the uses to which the three data bases for GP will be put. For each use, give a very brief describing access (updating, insertion, or retrieval) to each relevant conceptual data base file. With insertion/updating state when debits and credits are involved, and check on compliance with double-entry bookkeeping practice.
4. In some detail, give the procedure for handling an order from a customer for quantities of a number of different unit types. Show how the data base will be used for generating documentation for release, shipping, and invoicing of the goods ordered.
5. In both the accounts payable and accounts receivable conceptual files we could have a TOTAL field giving the total sum owing or owed on an order for parts or units (respectively). Discuss the pros and cons here in terms of functional dependencies.
6. The journal entry number fields (JE#) can be used to link all three data bases with relationships. Discuss (and check out) these relationships in terms of possible connection traps.
7. Design a system for tracking parts through manufacturing to finished goods, so that there are no credit/debit mis-

matches in theory for the entire accounting system for the firm. Design a manufacturing data base as well for the data involved, with any necessary modifications to the other data bases. [Time-consuming project].

8. Referring to the file LEDGER-ACCOUNTS in Figure 4.9, solve the problem of the relationship between asset accounts and accumulated depreciation accounts without using the additional field P-ACC#. Use the files of Figure 4.8 plus some modifications.

9. Referring to Figure 4.6, there is a redundant 1:n relationship shown, which if implemented would lead to either an undesirable functional dependency or inconsistency or both, depending on the method of implementation. Identify the relationship, and explain what could go wrong.

FIVE

American Electric, Inc.

American Electric, Inc., (or AE) is one of the nations leading manufacturers of electrical and electronic equipment. Although its annual revenue in excess of $10 billion is still small in comparison with such giants as General Electric, it is no pigmy. Its workforce exceeds 50,000 with a total payroll in excess of $2.5 billion. AE is organized into divisions, with each division concentrating on a particular type of product, for example, the Motors Division, the Power Division, the Nuclear Energy Division, and so on. It is the Motors Division that interests us in this case analysis.

The Motors Division of AE manufactures and distributes a wide range of electric motors. The division consists of a division headquarters in San Francisco with four manufacturing plants on the west coast, one in Los Angeles, one in San Jose, one in Portland, and one in Seattle. The Motors Division used to be an independent firm called Pacific Motors, before being taken over by AE and integrated into that company. After the takeover, the Pacific Motors headquarters in San Francisco became the AE Motors Division headquarters. Many of the former executives of Pacific Motors remained with the division after the takeover, with the result that the Motors Division retained much of its former independence. For example, its accounting system is independent of AE's system. At the end of each fiscal year, the Motor Division's income statement and balance sheet are simply forwarded to corporate headquarters in Hudson, New York, where they are consolidated with the results from other divisions to produce the final financial statement for the firm.

The Motors Division make motors, lots of them, in about 250 varieties, ranging from small motors to power an electric toothbrush, to large motors to power industrial machinery. Small motors are made in the Portland Plant, very large motors are made in the Los Angeles plant, and medium sized motors in the Seattle and San Jose plants. The division uses some 100 warehouses, scattered over the continent, for distribution of the motors. There are a similar number of sales offices, some of which are located at the same site as a warehouse.

At each plant, there is not only assembly of motors in a variety of production lines, but also part fabrication—that is, manufacture of many (but not all) of the parts that go into the construction of the motors. A part manufactured at a given plant might be used in a number of different motor types at that plant, and it might even be used in motor types manufactured at another plant. This is especially true of the San Jose and Seattle plants, which both make medium size motors. It is rare for a part made at the Los Angeles plant (large motors) to be used at the Portland plant (small motors).

Each plant also does its own engineering: research, experimental development, and design of new motor types. The Engineering Department at each plant relies heavily on information coming back from marketing for determining what types of motor should be developed in order to retain and even expand market share. In addition, division scientists are constantly scanning the literature for advances made elsewhere that could be used to improve the designs of existing motor types. Some years ago there was talk at division headquarters about setting up a Motors Research Laboratory to serve all four plants. However, corporate executives in Hudson were opposed to the plan, arguing successfully that the scientists would be better able to keep their feet on the ground if they worked closed to design and manufacturing in the division's four plants. Some scientists left the company to work for the arch rival General Electric, after the announcement about cancellation of the central research laboratory (which was to be located just outside Portland, convenient to desirable recreational facilities).

Data processing at the Motors Division was unfortunately something of a hodge-podge, and essentially most of the systems dated back to the time when the division was Pacific Motors. The then president of Pacific Motors, John Spin, was an electrical engineer who knew motors, and he had no interest in computers beyond the motors that powered the disks and printers. Essentially, if it didn't rotate or oscillate, he wasn't interested. As a result, here was no central direction from top management for the development of data processing at Pacific Motors. Systems developed independently at each plant and at Pacific Motors headquarters to meet needs that were pressing at the time. There was no integrated development and no use of data base systems.

After the takeover and integration into AE, top management attention at division headquarters continued to focus on motors and not on software systems for the smooth running of the firm. Management's attitude was that the motors came first and that if the motors were no good, all the software systems in the world would not help.

But as time went on, the poor state of data processing became increasingly obvious and embarrassing, not only to division management, but also to corporate management in New York. Sales were being lost due to poor record keeping and processing with respect to orders, back orders, invoicing, accounts receivables, and so on. Each plant had its own system for order processing, for invoicing, for handling cash receipts, and for accounts receivable. In each case, conventional file processing was used, and there was often duplication of data, as one plant dealt with the same customers as another plant. In addition, the lack of any integrated data processing for the division meant that each plant had its own sales offices and warehouses, although this was something that division management was not proud of and tried to hide from corporate management in New York.

After an incident where it had proven impossible to get a figure from San Francisco about delinquent accounts receivable, corporate management decided that enough was enough. Corporate management finally decided that it not only wanted the world's best motors, it also wanted first-rate organization at the Motors Division. Management hired a team of management consultants that was dispatched to San Francisco with instructions to come up with recommendations on how to improve organizational efficiency at the Motors Division.

The consulting team contained experts on data base management. The team's mandate was not just to come up with a loose set of recommendations, but a set of detailed recommendations that could be implemented. The level of detail even included outline design of any data bases that were needed. One member of the team was our old friend Sarah Didjet, who had married and moved to New York some years earlier, and was now working for the management consulting firm (Pember & Penny International, Inc.) hired by AE to investigate the Motors Division. Sarah had developed a reputation for being able to see the woods despite the trees, and had proved invaluable to her employer when dealing with the corporate wide impact of computer systems and data bases. In fact, she was the key technical member of the team. The others were accountants, one systems software and hardware person, and two people who could best be described as corporate negotiators with the charm of diplomats. The negotiators were Jack Cherome and Jill Cardin. The systems software man was Peter Bight. The accountants were Mary Assette and Jerry Dette. Despite their very different but complementary skills, the consulting firm had employed the latest psychological testing techniques to ensure a team whose members were highly compatible with each other, so that internal conflicts within the team were either unlikely to arise or would be quickly resolved to everyone's satisfaction.

On arrival on the west coast, the team set up a base for operations at the Ramonda Inn at Fisherman's Wharf in San Francisco. They then spent three days at each of the four plants, talking to executives and observing procedures and systems. They looked at manufacturing, at engineering, and particularly at marketing, order fulfillment, inventory, invoicing, and accounts receivable at each plant. Then they went to division headquarters and spent a week talking to management about the existing systems and how management perceived them.

At the end of this period, the members of the team held a meeting to review their findings and to prepare an initial plan of action. There was broad agreement. The problem was fragmentation of data processing, primarily with respect to invoicing, cash receipts, order fulfillment, inventory, and accounts receivable. There was much fragmentation in the accounting system as well, but it was felt that the reform of this system could be left till later and that it could be handled best by a team of accountants. However, as Mary Assette pointed out, it was important that whatever system they designed for integrated orders, invoicing, cash receipts, and accounts receivable processing, should be designed so that it could easily interface with a later, more comprehensive system involving all accounting procedures—that is, a computerized accounting system.

Sarah Didjet then pointed out that although this was desirable, it was very difficult to do even with a relatively shallow design for both the integrated order system and the comprehensive accounting system. This would pinpoint all the important interfaces. The shallow design for the accounting system would not be taken further, but it would be kept as a guide for the accounting team who at some point in the future (currently unforeseeable) would design the in-depth accounting system. In the meantime, Sarah and her colleagues would proceed immediately with an in-depth design for the integrated order system.

The corporate negotiators (Jack Cherome and Jill Cardin), who so far had not said much, then in turn made points about the kind of people they had to deal with and about the kind of resistance and objections they could expect a detailed proposal for the integrated order system to encounter. Jill suggested that they include certain key systems design people from the Motors Division in the design effort. The people Jill suggested had both weight in the organization, were frustrated by the way things were currently, and had personalities that lent themselves cooperation with the Pember & Penny team. These people were John Carry, senior systems analyst in Portland, Jenny Sutherland, data processing manager in Los Angeles, and Paul Akron, senior systems programmer in San Jose. There was nobody at the Seattle plant who seemed to fit in. The senior accountant at Motors Division headquarters in San Francisco, David Dearing, could also be counted on for support for the new system.

As the day wore on, and the meeting progressed, the team strategy began to solidify, and the various members agreed to take on specific tasks. The details of what each team member was to do and of what was actually done are too involved for discussion here. But essentially a combined design/selling/seduction job would go on. As far as the design end of things was concerned, it was Sarah Didjet who was the key person, with assistance, as required, from Jill Assette for the shallow accounting system design and from both Jerry Dette (the accountant) and Peter Bight (the system software specialist) for the in-depth integrated order system. The diplomats, Peter Cherome and Jill Cardin, would help arrange meetings with those key Motors Division people (John Carry, Jenny Sutherland, Paul Akron, and David Dearing). Even though the bulk of the design work would be done by Sarah, the diplomats would work to foster a strong impression that the work was really the result of ideas from those key Motors Division people and that Sarah was really doing only the clerical work of tying things together. The Pember & Penny team members knew their job. They knew that a final recommendation to AE top management in New York that met with strong resistance from the Motors Division was not what was wanted. The recommendation not only had to be a good one, it had to be politically digestible by Motors Division people.

As the meeting broke up, Sarah remembered reading in a data base textbook that although there are many technical problems in data base design, with any sizable business organization, the real problems are political. She was glad she had the diplomats, Peter Cherome and Jill Cardin, to help, for she knew that her own skills just did not stretch into the domain of goal-oriented corporate diplomacy and politics. Her strengths were in understanding overall corporate systems, understanding them in terms of entities and associated processes and activities, and also knowing the technology of data base management. In her younger days, she had thought that people like Jack Cherome and Jill Cardin contributed little in the great scheme of things. She understood now that they provided the lubrication to permit new systems and methods to displace the old.

The Design Steps

The design project at the Motors Division lasted almost seven months, although the work was 95% complete at the end of six months. The remaining month was spent attempting to finalize the level of detail to which the design would go. Readers should remember that the Pember & Penny team's mission was to develop a detailed recommendation—that is, a fairly detailed design for an integrated order processing, cash receipts, inventory, invoicing, and accounts receivable system for the Motors Division of AE.

Prior to beginning the design work, Sarah and her colleagues were installed in offices of the Motor Division headquarters. The first task was a data/process matrix for all processes and entities involved in the overall accounting system and the systems for processing orders, generating invoices, managing inventory, managing cash receipts, and accounts receivable. The entities were arranged along the vertical side of the matrix and the processes along the horizontal side. Sarah drew up this matrix following interviews and telephone calls to everyone involved in the processes. When a process was not part of the general accounting system, it was further divided into activities, which were used to refine the horizontal side of the matrix. For example, consider the process called invoice generation. This process breaks down into the following activities:

▼ Assemble transactions
▼ Prepare updated list of customers
▼ Prepare updated list of products (motor types)
▼ Prepare register (list) of all invoice and credit transactions in batch
▼ Print invoice documents
▼ Print Back order report
▼ Print accounts receivable summary report

Thus the matrix really is a data/activities matrix, showing what activities any item of data is involved in any activity.

The next step was to attempt to group the data items and processes (or activities) into two major groups, those involving the accounting system in general and those involving orders, inventory, cash, and accounts receivable. This was very difficult to do, and Sarah came up with many initial groupings that had to be rejected. Each time she decided upon a division of the matrix, there were loose ends. Each time she discussed the problem with people involved in the activities or processes, Sarah discovered new difficulties, data, or activities that she had not taken into account. But in the end a suitable division was decided upon, which Sarah formally documented. As we mentioned earlier, she did this so that at some later time, an integrated accounting system, with one or more data bases, could be readily integrated with the order system and data base that was needed now. This was classical top-down design.

The next step was the design of a preliminary data base using the data (and processes) connected with the order/inventory/cash/accounts receivable system. This was not so difficult a problem for Sarah, as she had had a great deal of experience with data bases of this type. A case that readers should look back at is the sales data base (Figure 4.5) that Sarah designed for General Power. However, the General Power data base was for a company with only a single manufacturing plant. In this case, there were four plants and a division headquarters. This did not mean that new conceptual files were required, but it did mean additional fields were needed in most of the files.

We cannot give full details of this data base here, as the details are voluminous, as are the explanations of why they are needed. Readers can simply assume that the data base is along the lines of that in Figure 4.5b for General Power, with many additional fields, and some additional files [Of course, the file POWER-SUPPLY-UNIT had its name changed to MOTOR-TYPE.]

The next step was a walk-through of the design. Here the Pember & Penny diplomats really showed their skills. A whole series of design review meetings were scheduled with the key people from the Motors Division (John Carry, Jenny Sutherland, Paul Akron, and David Dearing). Sarah's design was not revealed completely at the beginning meetings, only parts of it, according to a carefully thought out plant. The idea was that the Motors Division people would feel that they had been largely responsible for the design. Thus walk-through were conducted with parts of the data base. Readers will recall what a walk-through entails. You take a process or activity, and follow the steps required for carrying it out, using the proposed data base. The data base should allow you to carry out all necessary updates and retrievals in a consistent manner.

As each part of the data base was considered, Sarah omitted the more obvious parts of the design at the request of Peter Cherome, so that the Motors Division people would have the opportunity to suggest the obvious. However, on quite a few occasions the Motors Division people did not suggest the obvious, but something entirely different, and even more appropriate than Sarah's original design. In addition, the walk-throughs uncovered flaws in Sarah's designs, which the Motors Division people often were able to correct.

All this took time. There was such a meeting twice a week for five weeks. At the end of each meeting, Sarah would modify the design of the material under scrutiny, and then she would make any changes to the design of the rest of the data base that was affected. So as the meetings progressed, the design continually improved, and the sense of responsibility on the part of the Motors Division people for the design improved correspondingly.

The next step was specification of all the programs that would be run against the data base. Sarah had most of the information for this from both the data/process matrix, and the walk-through meetings. She did not get down to detail specification of such things as the screens that users would see, but she did specify the kinds of input and output required by each program and the processing involved. Further meetings were held between the Pember & Penny people and the Motors Division people to review these program specifications. As with the data base design walk-throughs, many suggestions and discussions with respect to these program specifications, were put forward and in the end the specifications had the solid support of the Motors Division people.

The next step involved Peter Bight (the Pember & Penny software specialist). You recall that the Motors Division had four manufacturing plants along the west coast, with a headquarters in San Francisco, and warehouses and sales offices throughout the United States and Canada. Having a reasonably detailed design for a data base and associated processing program was a start, but you also had to know where the data base would reside, where the programs would reside, where the programs would execute, and where terminals and printers would reside.

Peter Bight carefully analyzed the physical situation. There were two major options. A central data base and associated program library at headquarters in San Francisco, with remote terminals and printing devices at plants, warehouses and sales offices, as required, was one option. At the other end of the spectrum was a distributed data base (and distributed data base system, such as INGRES*) with sites at headquarters and the four plants. Peter Bight was strongly against the distributed data base system. First of all, at the time of this study, in 1987, experience with distributed data base systems in commerce was very limited. A firm as conservative as the Motors Division of AE was not the place to try out unproven technology. The Pember and Penny diplomats, Peter Cherome and Jill Cardin, were in complete agreement, pointing out that the group of Motors Division people they had been working with were probably too conservative to accept such a proposal, and that other powerful groups in the firm would be resolutely against it. The other reason Peter Bight was against a distributed system had to do with plain old-fashioned economics. The major advantage of a distributed system lay in the reduction in computer communications costs due to data being physically located where it was mostly used. However, in this case all of the plants and division headquarters were located inside one geographic region, namely the west coast, so that the savings would be marginal. Peter was not just guessing. He had carried out quite a bit of research to find out. This fact, coupled with the greater cost of a distributed system, made the distributed option largely uneconomic.

Peter then concentrated on the central data base approach. He envisioned a relational data base system, such as Database2, with both batch and on line processing. The system would run under the teleprocessing monitor CICS (from IBM), so that the large library of data base processing programs would be available to unsophisticated users at remote terminals and could also generate output, in the form of documents, at remote printing devices.

Peter kept his feet on the ground throughout the evolution of this grandiose system design. A key consideration was the ability of such a system to handle the load. First of all there was the sheer processing load at the mainframe computer/computers and disks. To estimate the disk loading, Peter constructed a data base load matrix, showing data base storage files along one side of the matrix, and accessing programs along the other side. For a given file and a given program there was a slot within the matrix giving total disk accesses per hour (computed from number of program executions per hour and typical number of file accesses per execution). From the same matrix, Peter could estimate the number of mainframe machine language instructions per second that would be needed (computed by summing the number of executions per hour of each program times machine language instructions per program). From the total number of disk accesses per hour needed and the total number of instructions per second needed, Peter could determine what type of mainframe and what types of configurations would be suitable. Here Peter acted like an engineer, and he brought in both peak loading and the margin of safety concept. He constructed a data base load matrix for peak loading and did his calculations on the basis of those estimates. His results were also estimates, however. So Peter doubled his peak disk loading and peak instructions-per-second processor loading estimates. In other words, he added a margin of safety.

(The margin of safety concept is well-established in engineering. If you have to design a bridge to take a load of ten tons, there is no point in designing just to take ten tons or slightly more. The future loading of the bridge, which might stand for a hundred years, cannot be predicted. Accordingly, the correct thing is to introduce a reasonable margin of safety, and design the bridge to take a much greater load, perhaps twenty tons.)

Armed with his loading figures, which included a margin of safety, Peter approached IBM personnel about suitable machines for the job and was relieved to discover that there were suitable machines, although the machines in question were all top-of-the-line mainframes of very recent vintage. In this way, Peter was able to decide a number of reasonably suitable hardware configurations for the proposed system. And just to round things off, he was able to find some IBM- compatible computers from competitors that could also do the job.

Further meetings were held with the Motors Division people to discuss the hardware/system software aspect of the proposed system. There was a great deal of discussion of Peter's estimates, but these had been made so carefully and conservatively that nobody was able to find fault with them. A representative of IBM was also called in to give first-hand information about the capabilities of top-of-the-line mainframes. In the end the Motor Division people backed the proposal.

Finally, the team drew up a comprehensive report that covered the data base design, the specification of the processing programs and inputs and outputs, and several options for the hardware/system software specification (mainframe, operating system, data base system, teleprocessing monitor, and remote input/output devices). This report had some 250 pages and was prepared in sections by the individuals of the Pember & Penny team. As well as the actual proposal for remedying the order system at the Motors Division, the report showed, in outline, how a later accounting system could interface with the proposed order system. In addition, at the suggestion of the diplomats on the team, the report heavily emphasized the contribution of the Motor Division people, mentioning them by name at every opportunity.

The team report was submitted to AE corporate management in Hudson, New York. AE corporate management promptly dispatched copies of the report to key people in the Motors Division, to determine (a) if the proposal was reasonable, and (b) if the Motors Division people would be willing to implement it. Within a few weeks AE management in Hudson received word from the Motors Division president that the proposal was very reasonable. Not only was the division willing to implement the proposal, the division was positively enthusiastic about implementing it, and, if there were no objections from Hudson, was willing to get started right away.

There is not much left to tell of this case. The proposal was implemented by the Motors Division and worked well. Thanks to the margin of safety built into the proposal, the system has never backlogged significantly, even under peak loading conditions. The details of the implementation and the final system would fill a volume (indeed, the documentation for the final system exceed 1500 pages). The Pember & Penny people were not involved in the implementation, which was carried out solely by Motors Division personnel. However, Sarah and Peter Bight did continue to act as consultants. They interpreted the proposal where it was vague or ambiguous and recommended minor changes when circumstances warranted.

None of this is really relevant to this case. The important lessons to be drawn from the case are as follows:

(a) No one person could possibly design a major data base for a complex corporation, or even for a division of a complex corporation. It takes a team with both technical and people skills.

(b) A major data base design project requires the support and commitment of top management. In this case it was corporate management in Hudson, New York.

(c) A top-down design approach is necessary, so that later data bases and systems can interface easily with the data base currently being designed.

(d) Key people from the groups that will use the new system and also from the group that will run the new system should be involved in the design stage. Most of the problems in data base design in a complex corporate environment are political, and this helps to minimize the politics.

(e) Walk-throughs of any data base design are essential.

(f) Data base loading studies are necessary, so that hardware and system software can be procured or allocated to permit the proposed system to function even under peak loading. The design should use the margin of safety concept, permitting the system to function even if loaded well in excess of projected peak loads.

(g) A final report on any proposed new system should be prepared for top management; this report should emphasize the contributions of all non-DP personnel, as well as DP personnel who will later run the system.

(h) It is probably best for the implementors of the system not to be the same people as the designers, with the designers acting as consultants.

Questions

1. Give two examples of how lack of integrated data processing at Motors Division with respect to order processing could cause severe foul-ups.

2. Before implementation of the integrated system for the Motors Division, why would you expect that AE executives in New York might have difficulty extracting information about delinquent accounts receivable from Motors Division?

3. After implementation of the integrated system for Motors Division, how would an AE executive in New York go about determining information about delinquent accounts receivable at Motors Division?

4. Assuming a manual accounting system and the fully integrated order processing system designed by Sarah for Motors Division, how would the information from the integrated system be useful to the accounting department?

5. What kind of information would you expect to find in the CUSTOMER file that is part of the integrated order system?

6. Assuming that inventory for finished motors is kept at each of Motors Division's west coast plants, what would you expect to find for the fields of the inventory file(s) for the integrated order system?

7. What kinds of fields would you expect to find in the accounts receivable file for the integrated system?

8. Give examples of how people whose primary skills are negotiation and diplomacy can serve a key role in a data base design project.

9. It has often been stated that with large organizations, some 90% of the problems in data base design are political. Discuss this statement (about 1 page discussion).

10. Explain how a data/process matrix can be refined into a data/activities matrix.

11. Explain how Sarah was able to plan for the eventual construction of an integrated accounting system using the data/process matrix.

12. Construct a walk-through scenario for Sarah's integrated sales order data base for the case of the Portland plant selling ten motors to a Michigan firm, where six of the

motors can be supplied from the Detroit sales office warehouse and the remainder from inventory in Portland.

13. When specifying programs for use on-line with a central data base, what is needed if the program will run under the teleprocessing monitor CICS?

14. Discuss the pros and cons of a distributed versus a central data base system for the Motors Division.

15. Discuss the pros and cons of using IBM's IMS versus DATABASE2 for the central data base at Motors Division.

16. Why would a teleprocessing monitor be an integral part of the integrated order processing system at Motors Division?

17. Explain, using an example, how a data base load matrix can be used to estimate the number of machine language instructions per second that would be needed when the data base is being used.

18. How can a data base load matrix be used to estimate peak loading of the system?

19. Explain the margin of safety concept with respect to system load.

20. Why would you expect that one or more large mainframe processors would be needed for the integrated order system at Motors Division?

21. The Pember & Penny team used great diplomatic skill to persuade key Motors Division people that they personally were largely responsible for the design that was really the work of the team. Do you find this ethical? Discuss it. If you do not find it ethical, propose an alternative strategy with which you are more comfortable.

22. In the final report to top management in New York, Sarah's team drew a great deal of attention to the contribution of Motors Division people to the final design. Discuss this, and suggest and justify any alternative that you prefer.

SIX

Peryl-Links Securities, Inc.

Peryl-Links Securities, Inc., (or PLS) is one of the nation's leading investment firms, with offices on Wall Street and across the nation. The bulk of the firm's income comes from commissions on transfer of stocks, bonds, and other financial instruments, for the firm originally started out as a stock-brokerage firm. But following a series of mergers in the early 1970s, the firm became firmly established in the merchant banking business as well, with underwriting of new issues of stocks and bonds for companies, and also distribution of sale of newly issued government and municipal bonds. By the mid 1980s many of the new issues being underwritten and sold by the firm were in connection with the takeover of one firm by another. The acquisitor would issue bonds or other instruments through PLS, to get the cash to acquire the other firm.

The underwriting activity in connection with corporate mergers put PLS in a conflict of interest situation, unfortunately. For example, if ABC, Inc. was intending to take over XYZ, Inc., then ABC would go to PLS to get the financing, which might be obtained by PLS selling new ABC bonds at high interest rates ("junk bonds"). But that meant that many PLS personnel knew in advance of the planned takeover of XYZ, Inc. Since the takeover price for the stock would be higher than the market price before news of the takeover was release, these PLS personnel (insiders) could buy the stock early and make a profit, or what amounted to the same thing, either get friends and relatives to buy the stocks or sell the information about the takeover to others with the capital to profit from it. All this is illegal. But in the boom of the mid 1980s some PLS executives got carried away, and following investigations by the FBI and Securities and Exchange Commission, some of them actually went to jail.

These insider trading scandals hurt PLS in its normal brokerage activities, which still accounted for most of the firm's earnings. So in 1987, a major reorganization was carried out, which was intended to make it quite clear to the small investor that its stock brokers (or "customer representatives") were not in possession of important information that was being withheld from them, while at the same time it was being used by insiders and passed to important clients, possibly for a fee. This was accomplished by setting up a subsidiary of PLS, called PLS-Acquisitions Inc., located in a separate building on Wall Street. PLS-Acquisitions dealt with mergers, and its personnel had nothing to do with PLS personnel, and in fact, were forbidden to have any contact with them. Thus PLS personnel could not have any knowledge of impending takeovers. It remained to be seen how this arrangement would work out.

At the same time, in order to rebuild its somewhat tarnished image with the small investor, PLS management decided its research department should be improved, so as to give small investors the very best research information available (except for merger information, naturally). Securities research at PLS had always been carried out by experienced securities analysts. These analysts would pore over corporate financial statements, computing key ratios and making adjustments for anything that could be considered creative accounting. However, the information in the latest corporate report is not enough for judging the suitability of a stock for investment. Information in corporate reports going back some seven years is also necessary. Even in the case of corporate bonds, such information is also needed. A case history should illustrate why.

Penn Central Railroad Co. was the nation's largest railroad. But between 1968 and 1970 its stock fell from $86 to under $6 in 1970, when the firm went bankrupt. The bankruptcy was the largest in U.S. history, and shook Wall Street. Not only did investors in the common stock lose heavily, but all of the firm's many bond issues became worthless overnight. And these bonds were held by all kinds of investors, many of them corporations. [The company the author worked for at the time held $10 million of them, recommended by a leading securities firm!] One of the securities firms that had recommended Penn Central stocks and bonds had been PLS. Many of PLS's customers were badly hurt by the Penn Central Bankruptcy, and many more left the firm. Following the fiasco, which good securities research could have predicted, PLS management had decided to set up a really competent and thorough research department. It never happened in the 1970s, largely because market activity was light during that period, with limited commission income for the firm. But now in 1987, following the insider trading scandals, there was no reason not to go ahead with the expanded research department. [Incidentally, good securities research could have predicted the demise of Penn Central from the simple fact that the firm's interest "coverage" was only two times, instead of a safe five times or more. This means that the firm's income before taxes and interest payments was only twice its legally required interest payments; any adverse developments, which are always likely in the business environment, would have meant that the firm could not have paid the interest on its bonds, and thus would suffer bankruptcy, which is exactly what happened.]

In 1987, following the legal and physical separation of PLS-Acquisitions, the data processing department was primarily concerned with systems for managing customer accounts—that is, the day-to-day operations connected with the purchase and sale of securities on the open market. Information for the research department was normally acquired by manual means—from the corporate reports for the latest figures, and from securities manuals such as Moody's or Standard & Poor's for figures for earlier years. The analysts in the research department had often complained that they spent most of their time looking up figures in manuals and corporate reports and entering them into spreadsheets on personal computers for analysis. In addition, they complained that they were interrupted far too often by requests from the firm's brokers for information about a given security—information of a trivial nature, such as last year's earnings per share, that was readily available in the manuals, but which required time to look up.

What was needed, in the opinion of the analysts, was a comprehensive investment data base, with detailed information about securities over a period as long as seven years. The securities of greatest important were common stocks, preferred stocks, corporate bonds and debentures, convertible bonds, convertible preferred stock, warrants, and municipal bonds. The research department people and the firm's brokers all had computer terminals connected to computers at the stock exchanges for obtaining the latest information on current prices for securities (which fluctuated continually). The investment data base would contain fundamental financial and business information about firms whose securities were being traded.

This fundamental securities information should be distinguished from market information, that is, mainly current price and volume of trading information, available online from the stock exchange computers. The investment data base the research department wanted would contain fundamental information, with current securities price information, or market information, not necessarily available from that data base (although it would be nice if it were).

In addition to the investment data base, the research analysis wanted software that would enable them to effectively manipulate the data base. They wanted to be able to get full information easily on any security by entering a simple command involving the name of that security. And they wanted brokers across the country to be able to do the same thing, so trivial requests from brokers to the research department would become a thing of the past. In addition, the research people wanted to be able to have the computer scan through any appropriate part of the data base, or even the entire data base, selecting securities according to any criteria input by a researcher. For example, it might be that an analyst wanted to know if there were any corporate bonds paying more than 10% yield to maturity, not callable before 1995, and issued by a corporation whose income before interest and taxes was more than seven times interest payments on all bonds and debentures it had issued, and whose current ratio (ratio of current assets to current liabilities) was greater than 2. To carry out such a search using manual methods would be prohibitively expensive, and could take a week or more of an analyst's time. [In simpler terms, that request about the bonds is asking for bonds that pay a good rate for a long time from companies that are unlikely to default and go into bankruptcy. As we mentioned earlier, Penn Central would have flunked the test in the late 1960s!]

The ability of the system to search the data base on the bases of sophisticated selection criteria was a critical requirement for the research department. A collection of selection criteria is known as a filter. Typically, in the process of selection securities as candidates for investment, at least two such filters, two sets of selection criteria, would be applied. The first set would select securities that represented good value for the money, for example, stocks with either a good dividend yield or exceptional interest return. The second filter would then be applied to the securities selected by the first filter. This second filter would essentially contain selection criteria that caused selection of securities from firms that were in strong financial condition and certainly in no danger of bankruptcy. The final small group of securities selected could then be further investigated manually by the analyst who would examine news reports on future prospects, read footnotes in the annual reports, and so on. In the end, the analyst could make some solid recommendations for investment that would be circulated to all PLS brokers and customers.

Many different kinds of filters, reflecting many different investment strategies and securities types, could be constructed and applied to the data base by the research analysts. enabling them to carry out securities research of a quality that simply would not have been possible by manual means. The results of using these filters, combined with the analysts skill and experience in making further manual selections, meant lists of undervalued securities with strong potential for an excellent return. Such lists would be invaluable for the firm's customers.

In addition, if a customer of the firm wanted to know of any securities that filled certain selection criteria, the research department would be in a position to construct a suitable filter, and use it in a search of the data base. Construction of the filter might take ten minutes, and its use in the search might take a minute or two, giving a relatively fast response to the customer request.

The thought of such facilities was very appealing to management. The question was how to get such a system in place. The personnel in data processing had no experience in data base management, and they were so busy with the day-to-day matters in connection with the business end of the firm that they could not be released for the investment data base project. It was decided to call in a consulting firm, and following some research into the capabilities of such firms, the firm of Pember & Penny was chosen.

At Pember & Penny, the project was not considered to be such a major one, certainly not on the scale of Americal Electric/Motors Division project, even though, in terms of commission income, PLS was a very large firm. The agreement with PLS management was for a two stage project: first a design of the data base and associated software, and second, implementation and installation. It was felt that a team of two would be sufficient for the design job, with a decision about the implementation and installation aspect of the project to be postponed until after design work has been completed.

The Pember & Penny design team consisted of Sarah Didjet as the data base specialist, and Fred Funds as investment specialist. A third person from Pember & Penny, Peter Bight, a systems software specialist, although not specifically assigned to the team, was to be available as a consultant to Sarah, if and as required.

The project suited Sarah. First of all, PLS offices on Wall Street were only a few blocks away from Pember & Penny offices on Lower Manhattan. Sarah lived on Long Island, so that the PLS project meant almost no change in her daily work habits. She did not have to stay at a hotel, or anything like that, which was all too often the case for a consultant who operated nationally. The recent project at AE/Motors Division in San Francisco had been particularly arduous. Compared to that, the PLS project was very attractive, and then there was the lure and excitement of the world of high finance that was centered on Wall Street. As a result, Sarah became very interested in the project and was not only well paid for doing it, but enjoyed every moment of it.

And so, one Monday morning, Sarah and Fred Funds entered the Wall Street offices of Peryl-Links Securities, and spent most of the day talking to Steve Pickem, vice-president for

Securities Research, at PLS. Steve used a good deal of Wall Street jargon that was not familiar to Sarah, although Fred Funds seemed to have no problems with terminology and easily struck a working relationship with Steve. Sarah was bothered by such terms as beta coefficient, market risk, net current assets, quick ratio, return on book value, cash flow per share, and so on. She soon realized that she had better get a few books to read on investment in securities and on the fundamentals of investment, too. She spent the next few days studying, with the occasional question over the phone to Fred Funds, who was more than eager to share his knowledge with Sarah. Meanwhile Fred was studying some elementary data base principles and in return had a fair number of questions for Sarah.

At the next meeting at PLS, they dealt with both Steve Pickem and Paul Raeting. Paul was research director for the Wall Street office. As Sarah then found out, PLS had smaller research departments at its Houston, Chicago, and San Francisco offices. Whatever system was designed, it had to be available to the people in those offices as well.

After some short preliminaries, Steve Pickem went off, and Paul Raeting explained that he would be working directly with Sarah and Fred Funds in the design phase of the work and would try to be available as much as possible, despite a rather demanding schedule. By this time Sarah was much more knowledgeable about investment terminology, thanks to her study of some investment books and help from Fred Funds. She had already decided, on the basis of her knowledge so far, that the first thing to do was find out what kinds of information were needed by the research people and exactly what was done with it. In other words, she wanted some idea of the data/process matrix, although not in formal matrix terms.

It turned out that the conceptual files for the data base could be identified rather easily, without a need for involved data/process analysis. In a nutshell, following lengthy discussions with Paul Raeting, it soon became clear to Sarah that there simply had to be a conceptual file for each type of security traded on exchanges. There had to be a file for common stocks, a file for preferred stock, a file for corporate bonds and debentures, a file for convertible bonds, a file for convertible preferred stock, and perhaps a file for municipal bonds. The following outlines the kind of information needed in each file. Later we will see how the files interrelate.

Common Stock File STOCK

The following fields were found to be necessary for the file STOCK, and the list below can be considered as part of a data dictionary. Because some fields, such as REV (revenue), are repeated for data for each of seven years, beginning with the latest year, we assume that the latest year is 1988. Thus we could have REV fields REV88, REV87, . . ., REV82, containing revenue data for the years 1982–1988.

STKNAME   Stock ticker symbol for the firm, for example "IBM", or "GM". Primary key.

P   Latest weekly closing price

Q-HI   Quarterly high market price

Q-LO   Quarterly low market price

BETA   Most recent measurement of the stock's beta coefficient. The beta value measures the volatility of the stock, or its beta "risk," in relation to the volatility of the average price of stocks from the entire market. If when the market average moves by p percent, up or down, the stock also moves p percent, up or down, then the stock is said to have a beta value of 1.0. If the market average moves p percent, and the stock moves only 1/2p percent, then beta for the stock is 0.5. Similarly, if the stock moves 2p percent when the market moves p percent, the beta value is 2.0. In summary, if a stock has a beta of unity, and you have a portfolio of such stocks, the portfolio value will fluctuate with about the same amplitude as the market average. If you have a portfolio of stocks with low betas, less than 0.7, the portfolio value will be relatively immune to market fluctuations. Accordingly, it is very useful to know the beta value for a stock.

AREA   Area of business for the firm—for example, computers, pharmaceuticals, construction, cement, and so on.

The following fields contain income statement information. All field values are in millions of dollars, and apply to 1988.

REV88   Total revenue for the firm

EPIBT88   Total earnings, that is, revenue less costs, but before deduction of interest payments, preferred stock dividends, and taxes. In other words what the firm would make if it operated in a world with no corporate taxes and no debt or preferred stock issues (which for many purposes are equivalent to debt).

INT88   What the firm pays in interest payments on bonds and debentures outstanding in 1988.

PDIV88   What the firm pays out in preferred stock dividends, if any.

TAX88   What the firm pays in taxes

E88   Earnings for the common shares, that is, the funds left to the owners of the firm (the common stockholder) after all costs, interest, taxes and preferred dividends have been paid. Dividends to the common stockholder are paid out of these earnings.

The following fields carry balance sheet data, with liability side data first, followed by asset side data. All figures are in millions of dollars and are for 1988.

(a) Liability side fields

AP88   Accounts payable plus all other current liability amounts except for bank debt due within a year (held separately in field BNK88. Thus current liabilities for the firm are AP88 + BNK88).

BNK88   Bank debt due within one year.

BND88   Total value of all outstanding bonds and debentures.

PRF88   Total value of all outstanding preferred stock. Although in theory preferred stockholders are part owners of the firm, in practice they are more like creditors of the firm, just like bondholders.

EQTY88   Equity of the common stockholder, that is, total assets less current liabilities, bonds, debentures, and preferred stock.

(b) Asset side fields

INV88   Inventories of parts, materials, and finished goods, with the inclusion of the value of work in progress, such as a partially completed jet aircraft at an aircraft firm.

AR88   Total accounts receivable, including interest receivable, that is, interest due to be received within a year.

CASH88   Total of cash and liquid securities. Note that current liabilities in 1988 are the sum of INV88, AR88, and CASH88.

FIXD88   Value of fixed assets, such as plant and machinery, in 1988.

The following fields carry other important information that is not part of either income or balance sheet statements.

N88   Total number of common shares outstanding in 1988. This field is used to computer per share values. For example, earnings per share in 1988 would be E88/N88.

DIV88   The dividend per share paid in 1988.

HI88   The high price per the stock recorded in 1988.

LO88   The low price for the stock recorded in 1988.

The previous 18 fields, from REV88 to LO88, are now repeated with 1987 data, that is, fields REV87 to LO87, and so on for each year back to 1982, for a total of seven years and 126 fields containing the seven year data.

Corporate Bond File BOND

Each record of this file describes a corporate bond or debenture. A bond is a debt instrument issued for a fixed period of time with a fixed amount of interest payable each year. Bonds are normally issued in units of $1,000. If the interest payable annually is $80, then the coupon interest rate, that is, interest rate when issued, is 8%. However, the price of the bond on the bond market will fluctuate. If you can buy it for $800, you still get the $80 annual interest, and you will also get a capital gain of $200 when the bond is redeemed for cash at maturity date, for a total called a yield to maturity greater than 10% annually. Thus there are two interest rates associated with a marketable bond, namely the coupon rate and the yield to maturity. You get the coupon rate if you by it when it is first issued; later it is likely that you can buy it on the market at a price other than $1,000, giving a yield to maturity different from the coupon rate. Calculation of the yield to maturity is rather involved and is best done by computer.

Corporate bonds have usually both a maturity date and a call date. The maturity date is the date on which the bond will normally mature, with the bondholder being returned $1,000 per bond held. The call date is an earlier date at which, at the option of the issuing firm, the bond can be redeemed. For example, suppose that in 1982 XYZ, Inc., issued 20 year bonds at 14% coupon rate maturing in 2002, but with a call date in 1987. In 1987 the interest rates are about 8% for newly issued corporate bonds. The firm exercises its call right, pays off the 14% bonds, and gets the fund to do so by selling new bonds with a coupon rate of 8%. Thus the firm saves, and the investors holding the 14% bonds are deprived of that high coupon rate of interest for the next 15 years.

Although bonds normally come in units of $1,000, on the market they are quoted as units of $100, with $100 being par value. Thus if the market quote is 92, that means the price of a unit is $920. In practice, nowadays, a minimum of about 10 units, that is, par value of $10,000, is usually traded on the bond market.

All these considerations lead Sarah to a conceptual file BOND, with the following fields:

STKNAME	Stock ticker symbol for the name of the firm issuing the bond.
COUPON	Coupon rate of interest
DUE	Date on which the bond matures

The combined fields STKNAME, COUPON, and DUE form a composite primary key for BOND. Thus, in practice, XYZ 11% July 1st 1995 identifies the bonds issued by XYZ, Inc., at 11% coupon rate, due on July 1st, 1995.

PRICE	Current market price for the bonds.
HIPRICE	Highest price at which the bonds have ever sold.
LOPRICE	Lowest price at which the bonds have ever sold.
AMOUNT	Size of issue, in millions of dollars
RATING	How the bonds are rated by the rating companies, such as Standard & Poor's or Moody's. For example, if Moody's ratings are used, in order of best to worst we have Aaa, Aa, A, Baa, Ba, B, Caa, Ca, C. A rating of Aaa or Aa is considered to very safe investment grade bond, whereas Ca or C is considered to be a high risk speculative (or "junk") bond, where the risk of default is great.
CALLDATE	The date at which the company can call in and redeem the bonds. There may not be a call date.
YIELD	The annual rate of return, including interest income and capital gain or loss, if the bond is held to maturity. The data in this field can be computer from the values in COUPON, PRICE, and DUE. Thus COUPON, PRICE, and DUE determine YIELD, so that YIELD is functionally dependent on COUPON,

PRICE, and DUE. However, YIELD is more than just functionally dependent, it is computationally functionally dependent. Because the computation of YIELD is so complex, and because YIELD is frequently needed in scans of the file for selection of suitable bonds, Sarah decided to include the field and arrange for updating software to computer the YIELD values each day.

DEFAULT Indicates whether or not interest payments are in default.

Preferred Stock File PREFERRED

The preferred stock instrument is a hybrid, with some of the properties of a common stock and some of the properties of a bond. However, it is best considered as a kind of debt instrument. The shares are issued at a certain price, for example, $20, with a fixed dividend, for example, $2. No matter how well the company does, this dividend cannot be increased. It is fixed for as long as the shares are outstanding. On the surface, the $20 preferred share would behave much like a bond with a 10% coupon, and, indeed, the price of the preferred share would fluctuate much like the price of the bond. However, there is a big difference. If a firm cannot pay the interest on its bonds, it almost automatically goes into bankruptcy. But the firm has no legal requirement to pay the preferred dividend and in poor times may omit the dividend. To protect the investor from this, most issues have a requirement that any arrears of unpaid dividends be paid before any dividend can be paid on the common stock. Preferred stock is often bought by corporations because the dividends received are taxed less than interest received from bonds.

Many preferred shares are issued in perpetuity, so that they never have to be redeemed, just like common stock. Nevertheless, some preferreds have a maturity date, at which the stock is redeemed at par (the issue price). In addition, some preferreds have a retractibility date, at which date the stockholders can submit the shares to the issuer for redemption in cash. In addition, some issues have a call date, at which the issuer can, at his option, redeem the shares for cash. In practice this will be exercised if interest rates, and thus the dividend yield on stocks in general, has fallen very significantly since the date of issue. The fields in the file PREFERRED are as follows:

STKNAME	Ticker symbol for issuing company
RATE	Dividend yield as percentage of par value of stock.
PAR	Par value, or issue price, of stock.
PRICE	Latest market price of stock.
ARREARS	Cummulated dividends, that is, total value of dividend payments in arrears that must be paid before any dividend can be paid on the common stock.
MATURITY	Date on which the shared must be redeemed at part value for cash, if any such date.
CALL	Date on which the issuer can, at his option, redeem the shares for cash, if any such date.
RETRACT	Date on which the stockholder can, at his option, force the issuer to redeem the shares.
N	Number of shares of the issue outstanding.
NOTES	Character string field noting any special characteristics of the issue.

Stock Warrant File WARRANT

A stock warrant gives the holder the right to buy or subscribe to a stock (newly issued shares, or treasury shares) at a specified price, called the exercise price. A warrant can also be called a subscription right or just a right. Typically a warrant has an expiry date, after which the holder no longer has the right to buy the stock at the exercise price, in other words, after the expiry date the warrant is said to have expired.

As an example, suppose that XYZ, Inc., whose stock trades at $40, has an issue of warrants, each one of which gives the holder the right to buy one treasury share of XYZ at $55 any time before July, 1995. The exercise price is $55 and the warrant expiry date is July, 1995.

A warrant trades on the market and has a market price. If the exercise price is $55, and the market price for the stock is $40, then the warrant would likely trade for a few cents, since the warrant holder has only the hope, probably futile, of the stock one day rising above $55. If that were to happen the warrant would climb rapidly in price. In the example above, if the stock were to climb to $54, then the warrant might be worth a few dollars, as speculators bet heavily on the stock price going even higher. If the stock rose to $85, the warrant would be worth about $30, since the holder could get a new treasury share for $55, and then sell it for $85, for a profit of about $30, the price of the warrant.

The fields for the file WARRANT are the following:

STKNAME	Ticker symbol for company issuing the warrant
ISSUE-DATE	Date of issue of warrant.
PRICE	Current market price of warrant.
EXERCISE	The exercise price of the underlying stock.
EX-DATE	The exercise date.
N	The number of warrants of this type outstanding. This is important since it means that there is a potential for an issue of an equal number of common shares if the warrants are exercised. There would thus be an increased number of common shares, but not, at least in the short run, an increased sum of earnings. Thus there is potential for a reduction in earnings per share, that is, for dilution of earnings. A program searching through the file STOCK for stocks with certain earnings per share criteria, would have to examine any warrants issued by a firm that would otherwise have satisfied the search criteria, to see if the potential dilution effect of exercise of the warrants was serious.
NOTES	Character string field noting any special characteristics of the issue.

Convertible Bond File CONVERTIBLE-BOND

A convertible bond is a corporate bond with the attached right to convert the bond into a specified number of common shares. The exact number of common shares is called the conversion ratio and is a key parameter for the bond.

As an example, suppose that XYZ has issued 6% bonds at $1000 par value per bond due in 1995 and convertible any time up to exercise date into 20 common shares. The conversion ratio is 20, and will remain 20 (unless there is a stock split, in which case the ratio is adjusted up to 40) throughout the life of the bond, no matter what the bond price does on the market. If the price of the common stock were $30, then the value of the $1000 bond on conversion into stock would be 30*20, or $600, so that at a stock price of $30 it could not pay to convert. The bond would thus tend to trade at a price reflecting its value as a bond with $60 of annual interest. However, should the price of the common stock rise to $70, then the value of the bond on conversion to stock would be 70*20 or $1400, so that it could pay to convert the bond. If this were the case you could not buy the bond on the market for anywhere near its par value of $1,000. You would have to pay at least $1400 for it, and probably even more because of the potential for a profit if the stock goes even higher.

It is thus clear that the bond has a split personality. At low stock prices it behaves like a bond, but at high stock prices it tends to behave like the underlying stock. In the file CONVERTIBLE-BOND, the fields needed to describe it will thus include all the normal fields for a bond plus additional fields, similar to those for warrants, to cover its convertible characteristics.

Note that although the bond will have a specified maturity date, like most other bonds, the exercise date, that is, the latest date for conversion to stock, may be earlier than the maturity date.

STKNAME   Ticker symbol for issuing company
              [Same fields as in file BOND follow here]
CONVERSION   The conversion ratio, or number of shares of common into which the bond can be converted.

| EXERCISE | The date up to which the conversion privilege is valid. |
| NOTE | Character string containing information about any special features of the issue. |

The Convertible Preferred File
CONVERTIBLE-PREFERRED

Convertible preferred issues are much less common than convertible bonds. They are similar to convertible bonds, in that they have a conversion ration and exercise date. The conversion ratio gives the number of shares of common into which a single preferred share can be converted, and the exercise date is the date on which this conversion privilege expires. However, apart from the conversion privilege, which affects the price of the issue quite spectacularly when the underlying common reaches a price that makes conversion profitable for those who bought at par, the issue otherwise behaves like an ordinary preferred issue. The fields for the file are the following:

STKNAME	Stock ticker symbol for the firm. [Normal fields for a preferred stock follow here.]
CONVERSION	Conversion ratio (See convertible bond fields)
EXERCISE	Exercise date.
NOTES	Character string containing information about any special features of the issue.

Relationships

The five conceptual files STOCK, BOND PREFERRED, CONVERTIBLE- BOND, and CONVERTIBLE-PREFERRED are all related, with the relationship supporting field being STKNAME, which contains the exchange ticker symbol (such as IBM, or GM) for the firm that issued the securities. The relationships are illustrated in Figure 6.1. We see that we get a

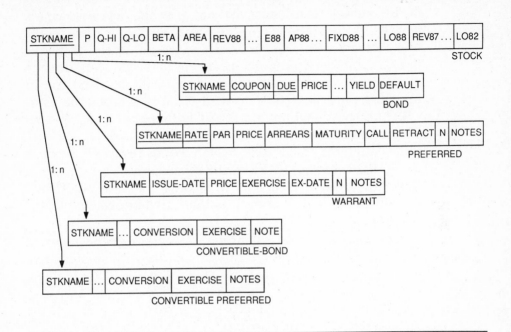

FIGURE 6.1. Proposed investment data base—conceptual design. Full details of the fields are given in the text.

simple two-level hierarchy, with a 1:n relationship between STOCK and BOND, between STOCK and PREFERRED, between STOCK and CONVERTIBLE-BOND, and between STOCK and CONVERTIBLE-PREFERRED. For a company there can be only one type of common stock, described in a record of STOCK. But there can be many bond and debenture issues, so that there is a 1:n relationship between STOCK and BOND. There can also be many issues of the other types of securities for a given firm, which explains the other 1:n relationships shown in Figure 6.1.

When Sarah had completed this initial design, she was quite pleased that the entities involved all fitted so neatly together into a simple hierarchical data base. Of course, she had not done it all herself. She had gotten considerable help from Fred Funds and quite a bit of input from Paul Raeting. At this point she got an idea. Except for updating the prices of securities, updating for the data base would be minimal. The vast bulk of the operations to be carried out with the data base would be retrieval operations. And these retrieval operations could be specified with SQL expressions, as far as she and Fred Funds could determine. So instead of the usual walk-through of the data base to determine if it could be used for its intended purpose, Sarah decided to build a prototype using ORACLE (with SQL) and a PC/XT with a hard disk. She created a data base with the fields shown in Figure 6.1, and with some help from Fred Funds, loaded it with 10 STOCK records, 22 BOND records, 15 PREFERRED records, 11 records for CONVERTIBLE-BOND, and 5 records for CONVERTIBLE-PREFERRED. Paul Raeting was then invited over to see the prototype in action.

Paul was invited to go through examples of the kinds of retrieval that would be typical. He started with some simple ones. We list some of them to give the reader the flavor of them:

1. When were the dividends for the past three years of the company XYZ, Inc.

   ```
   SELECT DIV86, DIV87, DIV88
   FROM STOCK
   WHERE STKNAME = 'XYZ';
   ```

2. What is the price/earnings ratio for XYZ, Inc., in 1988?

   ```
   SELECT (P/E88)*N88
   FROM STOCK
   WHERE STKNAME = 'XYZ';
   ```

Note that we are using the computational facilities of SQL here. The price/earnings ratio is the price divided by the earnings per share. Earnings per share is the total earnings (E88) divided by total outstanding shares (N88) in 1988.

3. What is the ratio of price to book value for XYZ in 1988. [The book value is the equity per share, that is, EQTY88/N88. The ratio of price to book value is a measure of how expensive the equity is. If the ratio is 1.0, then the price

reflects the value of the company as computed from the balance sheet. If the ratio is 0.5, the market is saying that the shares are not worth the value listed in the balance sheet.]

```
SELECT (P/EQTY88)*N88
FROM STOCK
WHERE STKNAME = 'XYZ';
```

4. What non convertible bonds have a coupon of more than 14% and a current yield in excess of 9%.

```
SELECT STKNAME, COUPON, DUE
FROM BOND
WHERE YIELD >9   AND COUPON >14;
```

Note that we identify a bond by the stock ticker symbol of the issuer, the coupon, and the maturity date.

5. What stocks sell for less than their book value and have a price/earnings ratio under 9.

```
SELECT STKNAME
FROM STOCK
WHERE P < EQTY88/N88   AND   (P/E88)*N88 < 9;
```

This is an example of a stock selection filter. The filter conditions follow the WHERE clause. This particular filter selects stocks that are cheap in terms of current equity and earnings. Notice that the work required to go through the stock manuals by manual means to make such a selection would be almost prohibitive.

6. What stocks currently have a P/E ratio less than the average, have a current ratio greater than 2, have less than 30% of the total liabilities in long term debt, and have had an earnings growth rate for each of the past three years in excess of 10%.

This retrieval involves a rather lengthy filter:

```
SELECT STKNAME
FROM STOCK
WHERE (INV88 + AR88 + CASH88)/(AP88 + BNK88) > 2
 AND BND88/(INV88 + AR88 + CASH88 + FIXED88) < 0.30
 AND E88/E87 > 1.10
 AND E87/E86 > 1.10
 AND E86/E85 > 1.10
 AND (P/E88)*N88 < (SELECT AVE((P/E88)*N88)
                    FROM STOCK)
```

It says a great deal about SQL that it can permit retrieval expressions (with the best implementations) such as this. Notice how the condition "Price/earnings ratio less than average" is specified. An inner SELECT-FROM-WHERE block is used to compute the average price/earnings ratio for all the stocks in the data base. In practice it would not be possible to retrieve stocks that satisfied these conditions without the use of a computer data base, since the calculations required for manual retrieval would be really prohibitive.

7. Retrieve the bonds with a yield of more than 9% and an interest coverage of more than seven times. [Interest coverage gives the number of times earnings before interest, taxes and preferred dividends covers the interest on bonds and dividends on preferred stock. In other words, if a company has to pay $10 million annually in interest and preferred dividends, then the earnings before such deductions would have to be more than $70 million. This would tend to assure even a very conservative investor that the bond was safe.]

```
SELECT STKNAME, COUPON, DUE
FROM BOND
WHERE YIELD > 9
 AND STKNAME IS IN (SELECT STKNAME FROM STOCK WHERE
                    EBIPT88/(INT88 + PDIV88) > 7)
```

This example shows how the relationship between STOCK and BOND can put to use in selecting suitable bonds. We can do this the other way round too.

8. Retrieve the names of companies where the cash, on a per share basis, less all debt, preferred issues, and current liabilities is more than 1.5 times the share price, and at least one bond issue has defaulted, or a preferred share issue is in arrears with dividends.

This filter is trying to select firms that are in trouble, but where even after all debt has been paid and all assets except cash are worthless, the remaining cash on a per share basis is still 1 1/2 times the share price. (This would be a classic case of buying a dollar for 66 cents.) The default on a bond issue, or dividend arrears with a preferred issue, ensures that the company is in trouble and a possible bankruptcy candidate.

```
SELECT STKNAME
FROM STOCK
WHERE CASH88 − (AP88 + BNK88 + BND88 + PRF88) > 1.5 * P * N88
   AND (STKNAME IS IN (SELECT STKNAME FROM BOND WHERE
                          DEFAULT = 'YES')
      OR
      STKNAME IS IN (SELECT STKNAME FROM PREFERRED WHERE
                          ARREARS ≠ 0.0))
```

In this example three related files are involved, namely STOCK, BOND, and PREFERRED. We use both the relationship between STOCK and BOND, and the relationship between STOCK and PREFERRED.

Design of Views

Paul Raeting was impressed with the sophistication of the retrieval requests that could be submitted to the system. It was clear that most sophisticated securities selection filters could be constructed and coded in SQL expressions. However, impressed as he was, he had doubts about the ability of research people and others, especially customer representatives at branch office, to use the more sophisticated SQL expressions involving nested SELECT-FROM-WHERE blocks. As readers will have observed, we demonstrated a few of these in the retrieval examples above. A further point that he raised was that securities analysts often want to apply filters in stages. For example, an analyst might apply filter A to all stocks and get a group of stocks G1. He might then want to try different filters with the stocks in G1, perhaps filters B, C, and D in succession.

Paul Raeting went on to give more specific examples of difficulties for personnel involving either nested SELECT-FROM-WHERE blocks or application of filters in stages. The solution to most of these problems was the use of views, which Sarah was quick to suggest. She went on to show Paul what could be done. We will give a few examples to show how Sarah used views in her proposed design.

The most common use of both the STOCK and BOND files, and the 1:n relationship between them, occurs when it is desired to select bonds that satisfy conditions involving fields in the BOND file and involving fields from the STOCK file that permit computation of how well earnings before interest, tax, and preferred dividend deductions cover interest payments. If nested SELECT-FROM-WHERE blocks are to be avoided with such retrievals, then a view should be installed that contains all the fields from BOND plus those fields from STOCK that permit coverage calculations. Let us call such as view BONDCOVER. With BONDCOVER we can simplify Retrieval 7. Sarah created the view BONDCOVER as follows:

```
CREATE VIEW BONDCOVER AS SELECT
  EBIPT88, INT88, PDIV88, EBIPT87, INT87, PDIV87, . . ., EBIPT82, INT82,
    PDIV82,
  STKNAME, COUPON, DUE, PRICE, HIPRICE, LOPRICE, AMOUNT,
    RATING, CALLDATE,
  YIELD, DEFAULT
FROM STOCK, BOND
WHERE STOCK.STKNAME = BOND.STKNAME;
```

The view BONDCOVER has thus the same fields as BOND plus the fields EBIPT, INT and PDIV for each of the previous seven years. Using this relation, the user will be able to check coverage of interest payments by earnings before deductions (EBIPTn) for any or all of the previous seven years without having recourse to nested SELECT-FROM- WHERE blocks. The following is similar to Retrieval 7, given earlier, but this time using BONDCOVER and coverage for two years.

7a. Retrieve the bonds with a yield of more than 9% and an interest coverage in both 1988 and 1987 or more than seven times.

```
SELECT STKNAME COUPON DUE
FROM BONDCOVER
WHERE YIELD > 9
  AND EBIPT88/(INT88 + PDIV88) > 7
  AND EBIPT77/(INT87 + PDIV87) > 7;
```

This is clearly much simpler, and most users familiar with securities analysis would be expected to have little trouble with it. Paul Raeting was very impressed, as Sarah demonstrated the facility in practice.

Sarah then got a list of all reasonably common types of retrieval involving more than one conceptual files (base table), and designed views to that they could all be handled by SQL expressions involving a single SELECT-FROM-WHERE block.

As far as two stage and three stage use of filters was concerned, Sarah's first inclination was to use a view for the results of the first filter and then have the next filter apply to this view. But on second thoughts, she came to the conclusion that this would be an awkward solution, since view creation would normally be under the control of the data base administrator. In the normal course of securities analysis work, researchers might construct hundreds of views in a single day for multistage application of filters. It would hardly be a workable solution if the data base administrator had to be involved in the construction of every view required.

On consideration of the problem, Sarah remembered that DB2 and ORACLE both provide for personal data base creation by extraction of data from the main data base. Why not place the results of application of the first filter to the data base into such a personal data base? She demonstrated this technique as follows for Paul Raeting, in order to get his reaction. Suppose that we have two filters to apply to the file STOCK. As is typical of the way these things are done, let us suppose that the first filter selects stocks that are good value for money, using the following conditions:

(a) Price/earnings ratio less than 10.
(b) Dividend yield more than 8%.
(c) Price less than book value.
(d) Last year's earnings growth rate greater than 7%.

A wide variety of second stage filters could then be applied to the stocks retrieved by the first filter. These second stage filters would typically select the stocks of companies that were in sound financial condition and not candidates for bankruptcy. As example could be:

(a) Current assets should be more than twice the current liabilities. [This ensures that the firm can pay its bills.]
(b) Total debt less then 30% of total liabilities.
(c) Interest coverage greater than seven times.

The user would create a new base table to hold the STOCK records that were selected by the first filter. Let us call this new base table STOCKCATCH. This base table has to be defined and have the results of applying the filter loaded into it, as follows:

```
CREATE TABLE STOCKCATCH
    (STKNAME                    CHARACTER(6) NONULL,
    P                           INTEGER,
    . . .
    LO82                        INTEGER);
INSERT INTO STOCKCATCH
  SELECT *
  FROM STOCK
  WHERE (P/E88)*N88 < 10
    AND DIV88/P > 0.08
    AND P EQTY88/N88
    AND E88/E87 > 1.07
```

When this is executed the records for the stocks selected by the first filter are loaded into STOCKCATCH. The base table STOCKCATCH can now be used with any of the second stage filters, for example:

```
SELECT STKNAME
FROM STOCKCATCH
WHERE (CASH88 + AR88 + INV88)/(AP88 + BNK88) > 2
    AND (BND88) + BNK88)/(INV88 + AR88 + CASH88 + FIXED88) < 0.30
    AND EBIPT88/(INT88 + PDIV88) > 7;
```

Paul Raeting was impressed with this facility, following Sarah's demonstration. He included that with the help of views and personal data bases the researchers and others would be able to undertake formerly prohibitively expensive research with great ease. He approved Sarah's basic approach. But it was at this point that Fred Funds pointed out another difficulty and Paul Raeting yet another one. We shall look at these in turn.

Accounting Data and Dependencies

The problem that Fred Funds pointed out had to do with nature of accounting data and the possibilities for inconsistency as a result. This problem shows up in two ways in the file STOCK, one of them fairly easy to understand, the other rather sophisticated. We will take the easy one first.

In the file STOCK there is balance sheet data for each of the seven previous years. We know that the two sides of a balance sheet must always match, so that for the data for any given year, such as 1988, the sum of the liability field values must equal the sum of the asset field values, that is:

```
AP88 + BNK88 + BND88 + PRF88 + EQTY88 =
    INV88 + AR88 + CASH88 + FIXD88
```

But this means that any one of this group of fields is functionally dependent on the remainder of the group. For example, if we take all the fields except FIXD88, then we can computer FIXD88 from them. Thus FIXD88 is determined by the other fields, and there is no need to store it in the data base. If we do store the FIXD value, there is the possibility that a value could be stored that would prevent the sum of the asset fields being equal to the sum of the liability fields. This would be a typical inconsistency caused by the dependency.

Ordinary data base theory says that such dependencies should be avoided because of the danger of inconsistency due to updating. Sarah discussed this with Paul Raeting and with another accountant at Pember & Penny. The consensus was that in this case there could be little danger from inconsistency due to updating, since once liability and asset fields were inserted into a STOCK record, it was unlikely that they would ever be updated. Thus the dependency was allowed to remain.

A much more sophisticated source of inconsistency lay with the consistency between the annual income and balance sheet data from one year to another. The most important technical point has to do with the EQTYn field and the earnings for common E(n-1) field. Essentially, the earnings for the common shares in any given year, such as 1986, less any dividends paid, go to increase the equity of the common stockholder at the end of the year. Thus if EQTY at the end of 1985 was \$580 million, and at the end of the next year (1986) the equity is \$626, the increase in 1986 must have come from retained earnings of \$46 million, provided the number of shares outstanding did not change (that is, N86 + N85). Retained earnings is earnings less dividends paid, so that we must have the following equality:

$$E86 - N86*DIV86 = EQTY86 - EQTY85, \quad \text{if } N85 = N86.$$

Thus the numbers in the fields for 1986 are related to the numbers for 1985. And, in general, the numbers for any two consecutive years are related.

If the number of shares outstanding changed during the year, typically because of an issue of new shares, then total equity must be affected directly. For example, suppose that the firm issued 500,000 shares at \$10 per share during the year. This would cause the equity at the end of the year to have increased by 10*500,000 or $5 million. Thus if we assume a share issue during the year at a price of S dollars per share. The following would then hold true:

$$E86 - N86*DIV86 = EQTY86 - EQTY85 - S*(N86 - N85)$$

provided the share issue took place at the start of the year.

As as result of these considerations, we see that the numbers for one year depend on the numbers for a previous year in a fairly simple way if the number of outstanding shares does not change during the year, and in a more complex manner if they do. Either way there is a dependency.

It was Fred Funds who brought up this issue. Sarah objected that the dependency was not meaningful as far as updating was concerned since the figures, once placed in the data base, would not be updated. But Fred pointed out that each year, the data for the earliest year would be deleted, and that for the latest year inserted. For example, at the end of 1989, 1989 figures would be inserted and 1982 figures deleted. It would be possible for the 1989 figures to be inconsistent with the 1988 figures, that is, one of the two equalities above might not hold, so that the data base would be inconsistent.

Sarah was inclined to say "Well, so what? The discrepancy will never be noticed." But Fred went on to give examples of how the discrepancy could be very significant, and he pointed out that if a wrong investment decision involving large sums of money were made on the basis of such inconsistent data, Pember & Penny, the designers of the system, might just be liable. At which point Sarah realized that the same was true for any inconsistency due to the sum of asset fields not being equal to the sum of the liability fields. And she knew enough to know that damages settlements in the Wall Street investment arena could easily run into the tens of millions of dollars.

To try to solve the problem, Sarah and Fred arranged a brain storming session with two of Pember & Penny's accountants. The accountants both suggested limiting the number of fields, so that dependencies could not arise and also inserting a field for the value of any shares issued or purchased in the year.

Thus, if CHGE86 is the value of shares issued (if positive) or purchased (if negative) during 1986, we have the equality:

E86 − TOTDIV86 = EQTY86 − EQTY85 − CHGE86

which is absolutely true. The field TOTDIV, for total value of dividends paid is also needed.

Sarah did not like the idea of complicating the data base by eliminating any of the income statement or balance sheet fields she had in her original design. It was at this point that she had an idea that everyone agreed to. The original fields in STOCK were to be left alone, but the fields TOTDIVn and GHGn, where n denotes the year, were to be added to STOCK. At the same time, insertion of new data for a year would be carried out by a program, and never by an SQL INSERT command at a terminal. This program would check that the above equalities held, following insertion of a new year's data. In other words, the program would contain a built-in integrity constraint.

This solution had a great deal of merit, since updating of the data base would be under the control of the data processing department, and not the users in the research departments. Thus this fundamental integrity constraint became part of the data base design, and the file STOCK in Figure 6.1 was modified to include the fields TOTDIVn and CHGEn.

Another updating consideration was brought up by Fred Funds. This concerned the price fields for the various securities, that is, the fields containing the latest market prices. The question was whether or not these should be the current up-to-the-second market quote, which would be very expensive to arrange, or whether the previous daily close or even previous weekly closing price would do instead. This was discussed with Paul Raeting, who thought most researchers would be happy with the previous weekly close and overjoyed to have the previous daily closing price for the securities listed in the data base.

On checking with the data processing department at PLS, Sarah discovered that previous daily closing prices for most securities were archived on tape each day by the PLS computer. The computer linked directly to stock exchange computers to obtain this data. The use of these tape files to update the price fields in the data base every evening would represent no problem. Another problem was solved.

Final Design

Sarah was able to present her final design to PLS management, in the presence of a large number of key securities researchers, at a meeting at PLS offices a few weeks later. The meeting lasted all day. The data base would be that shown in Figure 6.1, with addition of fields TOTDIVn and CHGEn in STOCK. The data base system would be ORACLE or DATABASE2, depending on cost and support from the software vendor. Updating would be by the data processing department at PLS, and would involve daily price updating, and insertion of new annual income and balance sheet field values as they came. The insertion program would use the integrity constraint discussed earlier. There would be four identical data bases, in Chicago, in Houston, in San Francisco, and in New York, where the firm's four main research departments were located. Users would be provided with terminals and the SQL language. A list of views to avoid the need for nested SELECTED-FROM-WHERE blocks with the more common types of retrievals was also provided by Sarah. In addition, users would be able to set up their own personal data bases to hold records on securities retrieved by earlier SQL expressions and securities filters. Furthermore, for some very common types of retrieval, retrieval programs would be provided, so that users did not even have to construct a simple SQL expression. For example, the request to retrieve stock data for firm XYZ would have a command STOCK XYZ, and the request to retrieve data on bonds issued by XYZ would be BOND XYZ, and so on. The last feature was designed especially for the needs of brokers, who simply wanted data on a given security quickly, and who otherwise might have called up a research analyst. The feature was expected to remove a great irritant from the life of the securities researchers.

There were many questions about Sarah's design, but nobody found fault with it. Indeed, there was a great deal of excitement about getting such a data base installed. The design was thus accepted, and the documents were formally handed over to PLS management by a senior partner in Pember & Penny. PLS subsequently hired another firm familiar with data base implementation and communications to do the implementation, and in early 1988 the system was in operation. Whether or not the system helped the PLS researchers to make better securities selections for their customers remains to be seen. An indication that it might not was the fact that other large securities firms, such as Child-Beanbody, B. F. Button, and Prudent-Handel Securities were all installing similar data bases. In the investment world, this is known as the efficient market. There are so many brains directed at buying securities when the market underprices them and at selling securities when the market overprices them, that for the current state of knowledge and beliefs, no matter how silly, prices of securities are set just right. But then this topic would get us into a case study on investment management, which is an entirely different topic.

Questions

1. Explain how a security researcher's time could be wasted by having to respond to trivial information requests from customer representatives in the field. Give a detailed example, showing the time involved.

2. Show how an investment data base would be useful to the researchers and customer representatives nationwide at PLS.

3. Explain the concept of a filter with an investment data base. Why do researchers use multiple filters in stages in their research?

4. Explain how Sarah Didget's knowledge of accounting principles could be used in the design of an investment data base, particularly the conceptual file STOCK.

5. Explain why researchers use financial ratios in the construction of filters. Look up some of these ratios in an accounting or finance text and give examples of how they might be used.

6. With respect to the income and balance sheet fields for the file STOCK, construct a more detailed alternative to that used by Sarah.

7. Using the investment data base design in the case, construct SQL expressions for the following retrievals. You may need to consult an accounting text for some of the ratios involved.

   (a) What is the current ratio for XYZ?

   (b) How many firms have a current ratio under 2.0.

   (c) How many firms are selling at price of more than 50% above book value.

   (d) What is the ratio of debt to equity for XYZ?

   (e) List the firms whose revenue has grown more than 10% in each of the previous three years.

   (f) List the firms where net current assets per share exceed the share price.

   (g) List the firms that have neither outstanding bonds nor preferred stock.

   (h) List the firms that have one or more bonds in default.

   (i) List the firms that have preferred dividends in arrears but have made a profit in the latest year.

   (j) Retrieve the firms with no more than two bond issues with a coverage exceeding ten times for interest and preferred individual payments.

   (k) Retrieve the preferred shares that have a yield in excess of 10% and are not in arrears.

8. Construct a view to permit researchers to deal with preferred shares and the coverage of interest and preferred dividend payments.

9. Discuss the dependency involved in the file STOCK because of the required equality of liability and asset sides of the balance sheet.

10. Discuss alternative repairs to the original version of STOCK to prevent insertion of new income/balance sheet data that is inconsistent with the data for the previous year.

11. Why is a relational system using SQL clearly one of the most suited for the PLS data base? Discuss the pros and cons of using INTELLECT in addition.

SEVEN

Securities & Exchange Commission, Washington, D.C.

The United States Securities & Exchange Commission, known as the SEC, was established by a series of Acts of Congress, beginning in 1933. These acts laid down the wide-ranging duties and powers of this all-important commission. The activities of the commission have had a fundamental impact on all aspects of the trading of securities in the United States, and even outside the United States. Among other things, the SEC has power over

(a) The trading of securities on exchanges.
(b) The issue of new securities by corporations.
(c) The method of presentation of financial results by corporations (income and balance sheet statements)
(d) Corporate reorganizations and mergers.
(e) How investment funds, or mutual funds, are set up.
(f) Trading by insiders, or insider trading.

Over the years, with the growth of the U.S. economy and the proliferation of securities trading of all kinds, the budget and staff of the SEC grew, and by the 1980's computers were being heavily used to help the SEC carry out its mandate.

An important computer system under development in the 1980s was EDGAR, which is a document data base system. At the time of writing, the system had not been completed, partly because of funding difficulties with Congress. The SEC requires that all corporations present their financial results annually to the SEC, on a form known as 10-K. The rules for completing 10-K are strict, and compliance with SEC rules here is an expensive undertaking for most reporting companies. Nevertheless, the result is that the SEC has in its possession a data base of documents containing financial data that has no equal anywhere in the world. And EDGAR is designed to place these documents on disk, so that securities researchers and investors throughout the United States would have instant access to this information via a terminal and the communications lines.

Unfortunately, EDGAR has not been without its critics. An article in *Business Week* in 1985 heavily criticized the proposed system for being limited in scope. The proposed data base was only a document data base, and nothing more. The authors went on to say that modern data base technology should be brought in to enable users to have access to a true investment data base (perhaps along the lines of that in the previous chapter, although the authors were vague here).

The commissioners were sensitive to this criticism but were probably correct in their view that you have to crawl before you can walk and that a document data base available on-line was a large jump ahead over the existing manual system, where you had to write to an agency to have a copy of a document mailed to you. Nevertheless, the data processing people at the SEC were beginning to have ideas about using data base technology to solve some of their problems.

Then in the second half of the 1980's a further impetus to doing something about data bases appeared in the form of a great merger boom, complete with all kinds of illegal insider trading, which stretched and the resources of the commission to its limits.

The idea that emerged from some people in the data processing department was for a data base to track the merger and acquisition activity of U.S. corporations. The subject of mergers is a complex one and just delving into the technical details of a single merger can be very time consuming. John Knowles, head of information systems at the SEC, thought it was time to do a preliminary design of such a data base, just to see what was involved. Eventually he was able to get the SEC commissioners to agree. However, the work was to be no more than a preliminary study, for which type of activity funds had already been allocated by Congress. Anything more than that would require a submission to Congress, and with the multi-million dollar EDGAR system currently the subject of a great deal of political activity in the Congress, the chances of funding for any other grandiose projects were slim indeed. The project had to be a kind of back-door unofficial project.

So busy were all at the SEC in the late 1980s, that work on the merger data base project could not be undertaken within the organization, and so it was decided to have a consulting firm look at the problem and report back. Because of its successful design of a large investment data base for the firm of Peryl-Links Securities, whose senior people dealt with the SEC on a routine basis, the firm of Pember & Penny was well-known to the SEC. As it turned out, Pember & Penny was the only firm to submit a bid on the project. Most other similar firms apparently felt that the job was too specialized and would probably get mired in political difficulties.

As we might expect, Pember & Penny assigned Sarah Didget and Fred Funds to the job. Sarah was very interested, following the job for Peryl-Links. She was even more interested because the data base involved looked as if it would require a recursive structure—something that does not commonly occur in data bases. The two best examples are in the field of manufacturing with bill-of- materials data bases, and in finance with data bases about the ownerships of corporations.

Mergers and Acquisitions

In the initial stages of the project, Peter and Sarah spent some time discussing mergers and acquisitions with Jill Joyne, the SEC's merger expert. They also spent a great deal of time looking up the accounting details behind mergers. We cannot go into all the detail in this report on the case, but the outlines should be instructive.

There are essentially two types of merger, namely the takeover or acquisition, which is by far the most common, and the amalgamation, although this term is not all that common, especially in investment circles. In a takeover, all or part of company J, the junior company, is taken over by company S, the senior company. Generally, S and J will continue to exist after the merger, with S owning only a percentage of J's stock. However, sometimes, if S gets 100% of J, J will be completely absorbed, ceasing to exist as an independent legal entity.

Some examples of mergers are (a) the takeover by Mobil of Superior Oil in 1985, and (b) the takeover of Rolm by IBM in 1985. In the first case Superior Oil was completely absorbed into Mobil, and disappeared as a legal entity. In the second case Rolm continued as a legal entity (Rolm is an important manufacturer of communications equipment). A more complex example was the takeover in 1987 of American Motors by Chrysler. American Motors was already controlled by Renault of France, who was selling its controlling interest to Chrysler. This example shows that a takeover can actually be a two stage operation, with first a divestiture or sale by one firm, and then an acquisition by another.

In an amalgamation, two companies, for example, A and B, merge to form a third company C. Here the original A and B companies cease to exist after the merger and a company C is born as a new entity. A famous example was the amalgamation of the Pennsylvania Railroad and the New York Central Railroad to form the Penn Central Railroad (which subsequently went bankrupt in 1970).

Usually the financial picture for the acquiring company, if there is one, changes quite significantly following a merger. The acquiring company has to pay for the acquired company. It can do this simply by paying out cash from its current assets if the firm being acquired is small and inexpensive. If the acquired firm is not cheap the acquisitor will have to arrange for financing. At one extreme it can issue new shares to get the funds, and at the other extreme it can borrow the funds either by issuing bonds or by a loan from a bank. In between there are all kinds of combinations involving equity, debt financing, and cash. A good accounting sleuth would be able to determine just what went on by looking at the income statements and balance sheets for the firm for the year before the merger and the year of the merger. Similarly, in the case of an amalgamation, the balance sheets and income statements of the amalgamating firms and those of the resulting amalgamated firm can be used to track the financial details of a merger.

Data Base for Takeovers

Sarah had learned long ago that it pays to do one thing at a time. So she decided to look first at a data base that involved only takeovers, where company S takes over company J. There were only two entities to be described, namely takeovers and companies. Each record of a file STOCK could describe a company listed on a major U.S. exchange, whether or not the firm had been involved in a takeover. The fields of STOCK would be similar for those used in the file STOCK for the Peryl-Links data base (see previous case), except that there would be a much greater number of both income statement and balance sheet fields, as well as the number of shares outstanding each quarter. As with the Peryl-Links data base, there were fields for this information for the previous seven years. The fields of the file are outlined in Figure 7.1.

The conceptual file for take-overs, called ACQUISITION, is also illustrated in Figure 7.1. In concept it is very simple, although it introduces a recursive or cyclic many-to-many relationship into the data base. The fields are the following:

SENIOR	The stock ticker symbol for the acquiring company.
JUNIOR	The stock ticker symbol for the acquired company.
YEAR	The year of the takeover.
OWNERSHIP	The total % of the common stock now owned by the acquisitor.
ABSORB	Contains a 'yes' if the acquired firm is absorbed by the acquisitor.

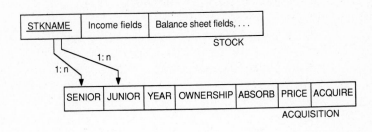

FIGURE 7.1.   Essentials of a data base for handling take-overs. Each firm is listed in STOCK, which is similar to the STOCK file in the previous case. Between STOCK and ACQUISITION there are two 1:n relationships, which means that STOCK is involved in a many-to-many relationship with itself. A SENIOR company takes over a JUNIOR company in a certain YEAR, having acquired ACQUIRE per cent of junior's stock in this transaction at PRICE dollars per share, for a total ownership of OWNERSHIP percent of junior's shares. ABSORB has the value 'yes' if junior is absorbed into senior.

ACQUIRE   The % of the common acquired in this action (must be more than 5% of outstanding common)

PRICE   The price per share paid by the acquisitor for the acquired share.

Before we get into a discussion of the recursive nature of the data base, some explanation of the fields OWNERSHIP, ABSORB, and ACQUIRE, is called for.

We can better understand these fields if we consider a take-over that does not take place in a single merger action, but in a sequence of actions, as follows. Suppose that company S is interested in acquiring company J. It first buys 25% of the stock of J in 1985 for $50 per share. Then in 1987 it buys a further 65% of the stock of J for $60 per share, for a total accumulation of 90%. Finally, in 1988 it acquires the remaining 10% at $80 per share. Then in 1990, J is absorbed into S and disappears as a legal entity.

Each of these transactions would appear as a separate record in ACQUISITION, as follows:

```
S  J    1985    25    NO    25    $50
   ...
S  J    1987    90    NO    65    $60
   ...
S  J    1988    100   NO    10    $80
   ...
S  J    1990    100   YES   0     0
```

From such a sequence we can see how the merger was carried out. Of course, many mergers will take place in a single event, such as:

```
S  J  1988  100  YES  100  $25
```

indicating that in 1988 S took over and absorbed J at a price of $25 per share. Notice that we can have a YES value in the ABSORB field only if OWNERSHIP is 100%, since absorption is not legal otherwise.

The data base can be used as follows. Suppose that we are interested in the takeover history of stock ABLE. Let us suppose that the contents of ACQUISITION are as shown in Figure 7.2 (neglecting the last three fields, which are not relevant to the discussion). We can find out all about the financial situation at ABLE, by retrieving the STOCK record for this firm. If we then look at the 1:n relationship between STOCK and ACQUISITION supported by the field SENIOR, we can get a list of the takeovers ABLE has been involved in. These are EELCO, FINECO, and GOODCO, as further illustrated in Figure 7.3. We can find out all about the financial situation for these three subsidiaries by extracting the STOCK records for them.

If we then want to find out about the subsidiaries of these three companies, for each of these we follow the same procedure as for ABLE. The result is the corporate ownership tree in Figure 7.3. It is the recursive nature of the data base relationship that leads to this tree, that is, the "explosion" of the company, ABLE. We could similarly get an implosion, for a company such as VEALCO, showing what companies own

SENIOR	JUNIOR	YEAR	OWNERSHIP
ABLE	EELCO	1985	100%
ABLE	FINECO	1984	100%
ABLE	GOODCO	1983	91%
BAYCO	DULLCO	1985	67%
EELCO	PAYCO	1984	92%
EELCO	QUEUECO	1983	100%
FOODCO	WHYCO	1982	25%
FINECO	YOUCO	1982	100%
FINECO	VEALCO	1981	95%
FINECO	DOUBLEO	1982	92%
HITCHCO	COLDCO	1983	100%
GOODCO	EXCO	1985	89%
GOODCO	WHYCO	1979	55%
KAYCO	WHYCO	1980	10%

ACQUISITION

FIGURE 7.2.   Each record of ACQUISITION describes the take-over of the firm named in the JUNIOR field by the firm named in the SENIOR field. The field OWNERSHIP gives the percentage of the firm in Junior that is owned by the firm in SENIOR as a result of the acquisition. Where the stock is acquired in steps there will be a record of each step. For example, if Able Inc. had first acquired 40† of Eelco, there would be a record for that. The later acquisition of a further 60† of Eelco would be recorded as the first record above.

stock in it, and so on. However, the tree of an implosion will normally be very narrow compared with the tree of an explosion. Indeed, in most cases the implosion will simply be a single list, such A owned by B, which is owned by C, which is owned by D, and so on.

Sarah and Fred decided to demonstrate this data base for the staff at the SEC, and so a small prototype was constructed on an IBM PC using ORACLE with SQL. The SEC people were impressed with the information that could easily be retrieved. They found only one fault, which fortunately could easily be remedied. This was a lack of information about officers of the firm. (The SEC people are very interested in insiders.) Sarah promised that it would be included in the next version of the design.

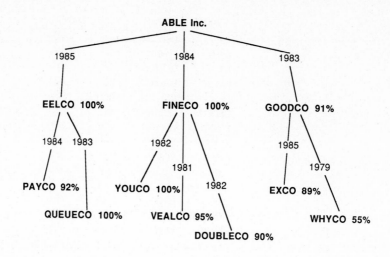

FIGURE 7.3.   Takeovers of the firm Able Inc. and companies in which Able has an interest. This corporate ownership tree comes from the data in the records of the file ACQUISITION (Figure 7.2). Further information about each of the companies involved can be obtained from the STOCK file.

The information about officers seemed easy to include. Sarah had originally assumed that it was necessary only to insert fields in STOCK for the officers. She soon discovered that no two firms have the same number of officers, and since searches would be conducted based on an officer's name, there had to be a field for each officer. And since the number of officers varied from one firm to another that would mean that STOCK would be a variable length record file.

After much thought, Sarah realized that the solution was a separate conceptual file for the officer service, called SERVICE. The fields of SERVICE are the following:

OFFICER	Name of officer
POSITION	Title of position, such as President, Director, and so on.
COMPANY	Stock ticker symbol for the firm
BEGIN	Date position was assumed
FINISH	Date, if any, position terminated

The data base for takeovers that includes this file is shown in Figure 7.4. From it the names and positions of all officers involved in a merger, and thus corporate insiders, can easily be extracted.

Sarah demonstrated this to the SEC people. She gave as an example the retrieval request:

Get a list of all officers of companies that merged with Fineco, Inc., in 1982:

SELECT COMPANY, OFFICER FROM SERVICE
WHERE COMPANY IS IN (SELECT JUNIOR FROM ACQUISITION WHERE
                            SENIOR = 'FINECO' AND YEAR = 1982)

The SEC people were very happy with this, although they did mention that they would like to see more fields in the service conceptual file. However, they anticipated the possibility of legal difficulties about possible invasion of privacy, and so declined to say what those fields might be, pending a thorough review of Sarah's final report by SEC lawyers.

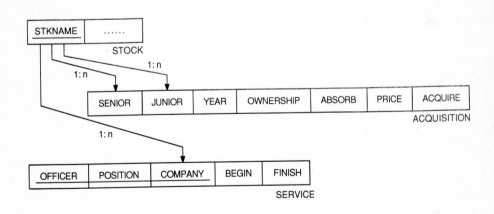

FIGURE 7.4.   Expanded data base that shows the officers of each firm, For a firm listed in STOCK there will be many officers, each listed in a SERVICE record. The BEGIN and FINISH fields give the period of service by an officer in a position. Thus it would be possible to retrieve present and past officers of any firm in STOCK.

Data Base for Amalgamations

Sarah then went on to design the data base for amalgamations. You recall that here firms A and B join to form a third firm C. A file similar to ACQUISITION is needed, and it is called AMAL-GAMATION and is illustrated in Figure 7.5. The main point is that there are three fields containing a company name:

NEWFIRM The firm resulting from the amalgamation (stock ticker symbol)
A-FIRM   One firm that merged
B-FIRM   A second firm that merged

Sarah was somewhat unhappy about the two fields A-FIRM and B-FIRM. Suppose that firms X and Y merged to form firm Z. NEWFIRM would get the value Z, but it was not clear to Sarah how it could be decided which of the two fields A-FIRM and B-FIRM should get firm X. In the end she arbitrarily decided that the merger firm with the greater assets listed in the balance sheet (the "larger" firm) should be placed in the A-FIRM field. She later discovered that nobody could come up with a better idea (although one SEC specialist did suggest that the firm with the larger revenue should be in A-FIRM).

The final step in the tentative conceptual data base design was to combine the data base for takeovers with that for amal-

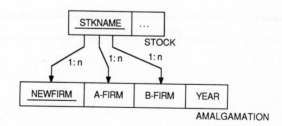

FIGURE 7.5. A data base for amalgamations. NEWFIRM contains the name of the firm formed by an amalgamation of the firms in A-FIRM and B-FIRM.

gamations. This is shown in Figure 7.6. It was clear that ACQUISITION and AMALGAMATION could be used separately with STOCK. Given a firm X, a user could determine from ACQUISITION which takeovers that firm had been involved in, and from AMALGAMATION if the firm had resulted from an amalgamation. It was the possibility of using both ACQUISITION and AMALGAMATION to obtain the entire merger history of a given firm X that then began to intrigue Sarah. After some though she saw that it was possible with the structure in Figure 7.6, although it was not possible to construct a single SQL expression to do it. Here is how it can be done.

Suppose that we want the complete merger history of company Z, that is, all mergers, both takeovers and amalgamations. First of all you use ACQUISITION to get the firms that Z has taken over. In Figure 7.7 these are firms A and B. Before determining what firms A and B have merged with, use AMALGAMATION to determine if Z is originally the result of an

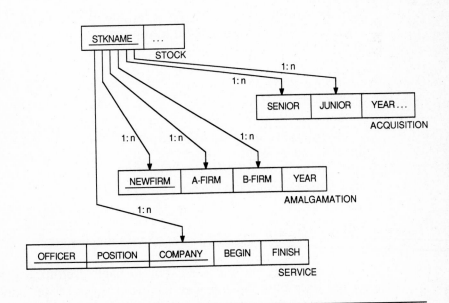

FIGURE 7.6. Data base for companies, take-overs, amalgamations and the corporate service of officers.

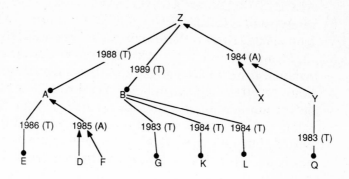

FIGURE 7.7.   The type of merger history tree that can be extracted from the data base in Figure 7.6. Company Z takes over A and B, with (T) denoting a take-over. But earlier in 1984 company Z was formed by an amalgamation (A) of X and Y. In turn company A tool over E after it was formed from an amalgamation of D and F in 1985, and so on.

amalgamation. Suppose that it was, due to the join of firms Y, and X. This is also illustrated in Figure 7.7. Now we can go to the next level of the tree, repeating the above procedure for each of the firms A, B, X, and Y. For A, we could find that it took over E, before which it was formed from an amalgamation of D and F. In contrast, B merely took over G, K, and L, and so on.

A demonstration of this was carried out for the SEC people. As mentioned, a single SQL expression was not possible, so instead Sarah wrote a program, which turned out to be quite difficult, complete with embedded SQL code, that could do the job. The SEC people were very happy with this.

Concluding Steps

This essentially marked the end of the basic preliminary design of the data base, which was what Sarah and Fred had been asked to do. A report was written, which showed both the data base structure and semantics. It also illustrated the main kinds of retrievals that could be carried out, both with SQL expressions entered at a terminal and with prewritten programs with embedded SQL. In the report Fred and Sarah also pointed out that such a data base, if it were ever implemented could also be the foundation for a U.S. national investment data base, that any user could call up from a remote terminal.

Such a national facility could help investors nationwide to make really informed investment decisions, and so help the proper utilization of investment capital in the U.S. economy, with all that would mean for the prosperity and well-being of the nation. But what the future actually holds in the form of national data bases at the SEC remains to be seen.

Questions

1. The SEC document data base system EDGAR is a real SEC development project. Try to find out more about it and write a brief report on its main features.
2. Explain the difference between a takeover and an amalgamation.
3. In the file ACQUISITION discuss the primary key.
4. With the file ACQUISITION how would you handle divestiture (sale) of company J by company S (assuming that there is an earlier record for the takeover of J by S).
5. Write a procedure for the explosion of any company listed in STOCK. English language statements will suffice.
6. Write a procedure for an implosion of any company listed in STOCK. English language statements will suffice.
7. Discuss the primary key for the file SERVICE. Why is OFFICER not the primary key?
8. Discuss ways in which the fields of SERVICE could be expanded to give more information about insiders. Discuss also possible breaches of personal privacy your extensions could give rise to. Does 'Uncle Sam'' have a right to file such information about its otherwise law- abiding citizens?
9. Discuss the relationship between STOCK and AMALGAMATION that is supported by the field NEWFIRM.
10. Give SQL expressions for the following retrievals:
   (a) What are the names and positions of officers involved

in any way with the firms that merged to form XYZ in 1988?

(b) What are the total assets of all the firms that were taken over by ABC in 1987?

(c) What mergers (takeovers and amalgamations) did XYZ engage in during the period when John Zing was president?

(d) What is the name of the president of the company that took over ESSCO in 1986?

11. Write a procedure for the explosion of any firm listed in STOCK, where the explosion involves both takeovers and amalgamations.

12. What additional fields might be desirable in the file AMAL-GAMATION?

13. How would you expand data base in Figure 7.6 to include stock purchases, sales and holdings by officers?

14. Discuss any dependencies you can determine involving income/balance sheet data in STOCK for the companies involved in a merger. (Note this discussion will require accounting knowledge of mergers.)

15. Consider and discuss what kind of a system and hardware would be involved for a national investment data base run by the SEC. You could assume to start with that 10% of the some 30 million U.S. investors would want to access the data base at least once a month.